The Law of Life Workbook

Project Editors: Pauline Salmon, PhD., Rhondeen Smith

Project Design: Lanika Wagner, Rupert Salmon

Scripture quotations marked KJV are taken from the King James Version

Zondervan NIV Study Bible (K. L. Barker, Ed.; Full rev. ed.). (2002). Zondervan.

This book is provided with the understanding that the author is not engaged in giving spiritual, legal, medical, or professional advice. If authoritative advice is needed, the reader should seek the counsel of a competent professional.

Copyright © 2023 Rupert Salmon

COURSE INTRODUCTION

Welcome to the Law of Life course, where you will learn about the fundamental principle that leads to freedom—freedom from disease, depression, and damaged relationships. Each of us longs for freedom from the problems that plague us. We hate being captive to the problems around us and within us. But we have a life experience that tells us that we might as well just give up, because such freedom is only a dream. It isn't just a dream. It can be your reality. Robert used the principles outlined in this course and applied them in his own life and relationships. As a result, he is now free from the autoimmune disease that was threatening to destroy his life. Anna used the principles outlined in this course and applied them to her own life and relationships. Now, she doesn't feel compelled to control her children or other family members. She has peace with her relationships. She has faced the loss of significant loved ones in her life with only gratitude in her heart. And her lifetime rash has disappeared. Carla used the principles outlined in this course and applied them in her own life and relationships. As a result, she is now free from the depression and guilt she was carrying from her divorce. Freedom is possible. It is ready for you, and this course is here to help you experience that freedom in your own life. In the Law of Life course, Dr. Sandoval will lead you through the unconscious lies that have held you captive to the truth that will set you free. Through the video presentations, the Law of Life book, and the thought-provoking questions and activities in the Law of Life workbook, your previous assumptions will be challenged, the lies you have unconsciously believed will be exposed, and you will be presented with a new paradigm of thought that presents to you new realities you didn't know where possible. You will be surprised at how simple, yet how profound, the Law of Life is. If accepted, it will turn your world upside down—so that you can finally be right side up. If this is your desire, then join us in the Law of Life course as we walk together to freedom.

COURSE OUTLINES

Chapter 1: Understanding The Cause Of Disease 5
Chapter 2: Learning From My Needs 14
Chapter 3: Deceptions Of Love 21
Chapter 4: The Law Of Life: Take To Give 29
Chapter 5: A Decisive Treasure 35
Chapter 6: Leaving Your Baggage Behind 44
Chapter 7: The Talent Of Suffering 53
Chapter 8: The Law Of Love...And Health 62
Chapter 9: Enemy Warfare 69
Chapter 10: A Love That Takes 76
Chapter 11: A Love That Values 83
Chapter 12: A Love That Surrenders 88
Chapter 13: A Love That Thinks Well 94
Chapter 14: A Love That Gives All 103
Chapter 15: A Love That Heals 111
Chapter 16: A Love That Obeys 117
Chapter 17: A Love That Overcomes 121

CHAPTER 1: UNDERSTANDING THE CAUSE OF DISEASE

As Christians, we understand that our bodies are a temple of the Holy Spirit, and we must take care of them. Disease is a reality that we all face, but we can better understand its root causes and how to prevent it. This study guide will explore the book "The Law of Life" and provide questions and key points to help readers understand the cause of disease from a biblical perspective.

The understanding of the cause of diseases is crucial for treating them effectively. In order to treat the cause of any disease, we must first identify what the cause is. Unfortunately, most medical practitioners only focus on treating the symptoms of the disease without paying attention to the cause.

To start, let's go over some key points:

- Everything we need to survive is determined by what we are, but each need must be actively brought in from the outside through our behaviors.
- If our behaviors fulfill our needs, we promote good symptoms, but if they don't, we promote bad symptoms.
- Beliefs are manifested in our behaviors and affect the health of our fruit (symptoms). If our beliefs about what we need match our actual needs, we promote healthy fruit, but if they don't, we promote diseased fruit.
- The roots represent our beliefs, and the soil represents our sources. If the soil is polluted, we will still promote bad symptoms, even if we have correct behaviors.
- Healthy fruit and leaves are the product of good sources, beliefs that match our needs, and correct behaviors.
- Humans can choose their sources, and the choices we make are rooted in our beliefs.

Here are some questions and main points:

- What is the difference between treating the symptoms and treating the cause of a disease?
- Can doctors always identify the foundational cause of a disease? If not, why?
- What is the analogy between a fruit tree and human health?
- What are the similarities between the symptoms of a diseased tree and the symptoms of a diseased human?
- Why is it not enough to pluck off the bad fruit and leaves of a diseased tree or treat the symptoms of a diseased human?

- What do the branches of a tree represent in the analogy, and what do they represent in human health?
- How can unhealthy branches be pruned to decrease the disease burden, and why is it not enough to solve the problem?
- What does the trunk of a tree represent in the analogy, and what does it represent in human health?
- What are some of the basic needs that humans require to maintain their health?
- How can understanding the cause of disease help us to effectively treat and prevent it?
- What is the source of everything we need to survive?
- How do our behaviors affect our symptoms?
- What do the roots represent in the analogy of the tree?
- Why is it important for our beliefs to match our actual needs?
- What does the soil represent in the analogy of the tree?
- What are the three things needed for healthy fruit and leaves?
- How do humans differ from trees in terms of their ability to choose their sources?
- What role do beliefs play in the choices humans make for their sources?
- Why is it important to understand the cause of our disease instead of just treating the symptoms?
- How does understanding the cause of our disease relate to our need for love?

Main Points:
- Treating the cause of a disease is important to effectively cure it.
- The analogy between a fruit tree and human health can help us understand that symptoms are just the manifestation of a problem, and not the problem itself.
- Behaviors or actions represent the branches of the tree, and they can either promote healthy or diseased symptoms.
- Understanding our basic needs, represented by the trunk of the tree, can help us maintain good health.
- It is important to identify and address the root cause of a disease to effectively treat and prevent it.
- Our needs are determined by what we are, but we must actively bring in what we need from the outside through our behaviors.
- If our behaviors fulfill our needs, we promote good symptoms, but if they don't, we promote bad symptoms.
- Our beliefs about what we need must match our actual needs in order for us to have healthy fruit and leaves.
- The soil represents our sources, and if it's polluted, we will still promote bad symptoms.
- To promote healthy fruit and leaves, we need good sources, beliefs that match our needs, and correct behaviors.
- Humans can choose their sources, and our choices are rooted in our beliefs.

- It's important to understand the cause of our disease to treat the problem instead of just the symptoms.
- Love is a universal need for all humans, just like oxygen, water, and food.

Scripture References:

- 3 John 1:2 "Beloved, I pray that all may go well with you and that you may be in good health, as it goes well with your soul."
- Psalm 103:2-3 "Bless the Lord, O my soul, and forget not all his benefits, who forgives all your iniquity, who heals all your diseases."
- Isaiah 53:5 "But he was wounded for our transgressions; he was crushed for our iniquities; upon him was the chastisement that brought us peace, and with his stripes we are healed."
- For as he thinks in his heart, so is he." - Proverbs 23:7
- "Do not conform to the pattern of this world, but be transformed by the renewing of your mind." - Romans 12:2
- "As a man thinks in his heart, so is he." - Proverbs 23:7
- "I can do all things through Christ who strengthens me." - Philippians 4:13
- "The fear of the Lord is the beginning of wisdom, and knowledge of the Holy One is understanding." - Proverbs 9:10

Other insights on this chapter for better understanding are listed below:

1. What is the cause of high blood pressure?
   - Vasoconstriction is the cause of high blood pressure.
2. What is the cause of vasoconstriction?
   - Increased activity of the sympathetic nervous system.
3. What is the cause of increased sympathetic nervous system stimulation?
   - One of the causes is increased leptin.
4. What is leptin?
   - Leptin is a hormone released from fat cells in the body that travels in the blood to a part of the brain called the hypothalamus.
5. What is the cause of increased leptin?
   - Increased fat in the body, especially central fat around the organs.
6. What is the cause of increased fat?
   - A positive calorie balance, which means that you eat more calories than you burn.
7. What is the cause of increased calories?
   - An increase in calorie-dense food.
8. What is the cause of an increase in calorie-dense foods in your diet?
   - Your taste, which is developed over time by repetitive choices.
9. What is the cause of your habits?
   - It has to do with your appetites.
10. What is the cause of your appetite?
    - It is the result of your human nature.
11. What is the cause of your human nature?
    - It is sin.

Key points to reinforce:

- Causes have causes, and each cause we find is caused by something else, until we get to the root cause.
- Disease, in many cases, is the result of a love problem.
- The foundation of God's law is His character, which is founded on love.
- The law given upon Sinai was the enunciation of the principle of love, a revelation to earth of the law of heaven.
- There is a divinely appointed connection between sin and disease.

Scripture references to include:

- "For sin is the transgression of the law." (1 John 3:4 KJV)
- "'You shall love the Lord your God with all your heart, with all your soul, and with all your mind.' This is the first and great commandment. And the second is like it: 'You shall love your neighbor as yourself.' On these two commandments hang all the Law and the Prophets." (Matthew 22:37-40 NKJV)
- "But he was wounded for our transgressions, he was bruised for our iniquities: the chastisement of our peace was upon him; and with his stripes we are healed." (Isaiah 53:5 KJV)

While illustrating THE LAW OF LIFE, We can use the analogy of a highway of health with two ditches on either side. Staying on the road ensures health, while veering off into either ditch leads to problems. Let's explore the factors needed to maintain health and how deviating from these factors leads to disease.

Key Points

1. Health needs include oxygen, water, nutrients, and warmth.
2. Deviating from the laws that govern these factors results in symptoms that indicate a departure from the law.
3. Symptoms are uncomfortable and help us to know that something is wrong and that we need to do something about it.
4. Disease is a more severe effect of deviation from the law with the purpose of getting our attention so that we can get back into line with the laws by which we function.
5. If we continue to deviate from the laws, we eventually cross a boundary called the point of no return and eventually die.

Questions

1. What are the health needs that are required to maintain our health?
2. Why are symptoms uncomfortable?
3. What is the purpose of disease?
4. What happens if we continue to deviate from the laws that govern our health?
5. What is the point of no return?

Reiterating Main Points

1. The Law of Life governs our health and well-being.
2. Symptoms indicate a departure from the laws that govern our health.
3. Disease is a more severe effect of deviation from the law and is an effort to get our attention so that we can get back into line with the laws by which we function.

4. If we continue to deviate from the laws, we eventually cross a boundary called the point of no return and eventually die.

Scriptural References

1. Proverbs 4:20-22 - "My son, pay attention to what I say; turn your ear to my words. Do not let them out of your sight, keep them within your heart; for they are life to those who find them and health to one's whole body."

2. James 5:14-15 - "Is anyone among you sick? Let them call the elders of the church to pray over them and anoint them with oil in the name of the Lord. And the prayer offered in faith will make the sick person well; the Lord will raise them up. If they have sinned, they will be forgiven."

Role of the Enemy in Disease

1. How did the Enemy cause disease in Job's life?
2. Can the Enemy cause disease in our lives today?
3. How can we prevent the Enemy from gaining access to our lives?
4. What role does sin play in disease prevention?

Key Points:

1. The Law of Diffusion states that substances dissolved in water distribute evenly throughout the water, so chemicals, such as uric acid, have essentially the same level in the arm as in the toe.

2. Energy issues in the nervous system can be the primary cause of disease, with chemicals, such as uric acid and cholesterol, serving as cofactors.

3. Our thoughts and attitudes can influence the signals sent through our nerves, which can impact our immune system and cause or prevent inflammation.

4. The nervous system can play a role in cancer development and spread, with our thoughts and attitudes again playing a key role in cancer prevention.

5. The Enemy can cause dysfunction and disease in our lives, but we can prevent him from gaining access by faith in God's grace, which leads to avoiding sin and living righteously.

Scriptures:

- 1 Corinthians 6:19-20 - "Do you not know that your bodies are temples of the Holy Spirit, who is in you, whom you have received from God? You are not your own; you were bought at a price. Therefore, honor God with your bodies."
- Philippians 4:8 - "Finally, brothers and sisters, whatever is true, whatever is noble, whatever is right, whatever is pure, whatever is lovely, whatever is admirable—if anything is excellent or praiseworthy—think about such things."

- James 4:7 - "Submit yourselves, then, to God. Resist the devil, and he will flee from you." 1 Peter 5:8 - "Be alert and of sober mind. Your enemy the devil prowls around like a roaring lion looking for someone to devour."

NOTE

NOTE

CHAPTER 2:
LEARNING FROM MY NEEDS

Through this study guide, we will delve into the wisdom found in the book "The Law of Life" and connect it with biblical principles, infusing the content with scriptures and a deep spiritual perspective. Let us embark on this journey of discovery, nurturing both our bodies and souls.

The Interplay of Basic Needs and Delivery Pathways

Reiterating the Main Points:

1. Our cells have needs that must be supplied (including oxygen, water, nutrients, warmth, and sunshine) to thrive. (Psalm 104:14-15, Matthew 6:25-26)

2. Organs and organ systems act as delivery pathways, bringing these vital elements into our bodies. (Psalm 139:14, 1 Corinthians 12:12-27)

3. Lungs bless us with life-sustaining oxygen, the stomach processes nourishing water and nutrients, the skin maintains warmth, the eyes and skin absorb heavenly sunlight, and the mind allows restful sleep. (Genesis 2:7, Psalm 107:9, Proverbs 4:20-22)

4. The blood carries precious raw materials to every cell, while the nerves supply the necessary energy for their functions. (Leviticus 17:11, Psalm 139:14, Matthew 9:20-22)

5. Love, an indispensable need, flows into our bodies through thoughtful contemplation, guided by the intangible spirit. (1 Corinthians 2:11, 1 John 4:7-8)

Questions for Reflection:

1. How do the lungs, stomach, skin, eyes, and brain contribute to fulfilling our basic needs?

2. How do the scriptures affirm the intricate design and interconnectedness of our bodily functions?

3. Reflect on the divine purpose behind the provision of these delivery pathways and the importance of recognizing them as gifts.

4. How can the integration of biblical teachings and scientific understanding enhance our appreciation for the wonders of our bodies?

The Importance of Right Sources and Actions

Reiterating the Main Points:

1. The path to holistic health lies in aligning our actions with the right sources.
2. Breathing clean air with abundant oxygen, drinking pure water, consuming nutritious food, and nurturing loving thoughts based on divine guidance promote well-being. (Genesis 1:29, Proverbs 14:30, Philippians 4:8)
3. Embracing wrong actions or relying on toxic sources can lead to disease and death. (Proverbs 23:20-21, Romans 6:23)
4. Overeating, hyperventilating, and exposing ourselves to harmful substances exemplify the consequences of wrong actions and sources.

Questions for Reflection:

1. How do the scriptures guide us in discerning the right sources for our physical and spiritual well-being?
2. Reflect on the connection between right actions and right sources in maintaining holistic health.
3. Discuss the impact of aligning our actions and sources on our physical, emotional, and spiritual states.
4. How can biblical teachings inspire us to make intentional choices that promote vitality and abundant life?

Recognizing Our Limitations and Embracing Divine Love

Reiterating the Main Points:

1. Our innate inability to create our needs humbles us, revealing our human limitations. (Jeremiah 17:9, Romans 3:23)
2. Love, an undeniable need, cannot be produced or manufactured by us but requires a divine source. (1 John 4:19, Romans 5:5)
3. The human need for love is universal, emphasizing our shared reliance on the divine for fulfillment. (Matthew 22:39, Galatians 3:28)
4. Our dependence on divine love connects our physical and spiritual selves, bridging the gap between body and spirit. (Mark 12:30, 1 Corinthians 6:19-20)

Questions for Reflection:

1. How does recognizing our inability to create love deepen our understanding of our dependence on God?
2. Discuss the transformative power of divine love and its impact on our overall well-being.

3. Explore how acknowledging our need for love connects us with others and strengthens our spiritual journey.
4. How can the integration of divine love into our thoughts and actions foster healing and wholeness in our lives?

Basis of Relationship Issues

Main Point: Frustration arises in relationships when we seek from others what they cannot provide, leading to unmet needs and discontentment.

Reiteration: Our expectations of receiving love from others often result in frustration because they are unable to fulfill our deepest needs. We must recognize that seeking fulfillment solely from human sources is misguided. Instead, we must turn to the true source of love, God Himself.

Questions:
1. Why do we get frustrated when others don't give us the love we need?
2. What is the problem with expecting others to meet our deepest needs?
3. Where should we turn to find true and unconditional love?

Scripture Reference: "Beloved, let us love one another, for love is from God, and whoever loves has been born of God and knows God." - 1 John 4:7

Whose Responsibility?

Main Point: It is our responsibility to seek and receive love, as God has provided an abundant buffet of love for us to partake in.

Reiteration: Just as it is our responsibility to breathe, drink water, and nourish our bodies with proper nutrients, it is also our responsibility to seek and receive love. God has prepared a buffet of love, overflowing with grace, security, truth, and acceptance. It is up to us to partake in His abundant love and make it our own.

Questions:
1. Whose responsibility is it for us to be filled with love?
2. How can we know that it is our responsibility and not God's?
3. What are some aspects of God's buffet of love?

Scripture Reference: "May the Lord make your love increase and overflow for each other and for everyone else, just as ours does for you." - 1 Thessalonians 3:12

The Buffet

Main Point: God's buffet of love is always available, while other selfish buffets offered by the world may bring temporary pleasure but ultimately lead to hurt and pain.

Reiteration: The world presents its own buffets filled with selfishness, offering power, pleasure, popularity, and possessions. However, indulging in these worldly buffets only brings temporary satisfaction and can lead to betrayal, abuse, and deceit. God's buffet of love, on the other hand, is always open, never empty, and provides lasting fulfillment.

Questions:
1. What happens when we eat from the buffets of others?
2. How can we distinguish between God's buffet of love and the selfish buffets of the world?
3. What are the consequences of choosing one buffet over the other?

Scripture Reference: "For everything in the world—the lust of the flesh, the lust of the eyes, and the pride of life—comes not from the Father but from the world." - 1 John 2:16

The Body & The Spirit

Main Point: The body and spirit are intricately connected, working together to form a living being.

Scripture Reference: Genesis 2:7 - "And the Lord God formed man of the dust of the ground and breathed into his nostrils the breath of life, and man became a living being."

Reiteration: Just as God married the body and spirit together at creation, our physical existence (the dust) and the spiritual essence (the breath of life) combine to form a living being.

Synergism

Main Point: The union of body and spirit is synergistic, where the whole is greater than the sum of its parts.

Scripture Reference: Genesis 2:24 - "Therefore a man shall leave his father and mother and be joined to his wife, and they shall become one flesh."

Reiteration: Just as a man and a woman, when united in marriage, form a synergistic bond that enables them to reproduce, the body and spirit together create a soul that is more than the sum of their individual elements.

Conflict

Main Point: Conflict arises from the dual nature of our physical and spiritual selves, leading to the need for harmony and balance.

Reiteration: As physical and spiritual beings, conflict can occur within ourselves. Our body interacts with the physical world, while our spirit imparts life and spiritual power. The soul, the conscious and aware part of us, is where the physical and spiritual unite.

Different Needs

Main Point: Our physical and spiritual needs differ, and our spiritual needs, rooted in love, are ultimately greater.

Scripture Reference: Matthew 22:37-39 - "You shall love the Lord your God with all your heart, with all your soul, and with all your mind. This is the first and great commandment. And the second is like it: 'You shall love your neighbor as yourself.'"

Reiteration: While our physical needs encompass basic necessities, our spiritual needs include grace, harmony, security, belonging, acceptance, liberty, righteousness, truth, and understanding. Love is the essence of these spiritual needs, highlighting their significance.

Nurturing the Spirit

Main Point: Our spirit has the power to guide and direct our physical body, choosing to prioritize spiritual needs over physical desires.

Reiteration: Through examples like fasting, we learn that our spirit's needs, driven by love and a deeper relationship with God, hold greater importance. The spirit's commands take precedence over the body's requests.

NOTE

NOTE

CHAPTER 3: DECEPTIONS OF LOVE

Love is a powerful force that shapes our relationships and interactions. However, in a world filled with deceptions and misguided expectations, it is crucial for Christians to understand the true essence of love and its connection to gain and loss. In this study guide, we will explore the insights from the book "The Law of Life" and delve into biblical principles to gain a deeper understanding of the deceptions of love. Through thought-provoking questions and scriptural references, we will reinforce key points and encourage a spiritual perspective.

The Gift

1. How does it feel when a gift you lovingly prepared and offered is rejected? Scripture Reference: Matthew 10:14 (The rejection of Jesus' message)
2. What is the difference between personal hurt and detachment when our gifts are rejected? Scripture Reference: 1 Peter 4:12-13 (Enduring trials and rejoicing)
3. How does human love differ from God's love when it comes to giving and expectations? Scripture Reference: Matthew 5:46-47 (Love beyond expectations)

The Heart - Human

1. What is the role of the heart in decision-making, and what criteria influence our choices? Scripture Reference: Proverbs 4:23 (Guarding the heart)
2. How does our value system and treasure affect our perception of gain and loss? Scripture Reference: Matthew 6:19-21 (Storing treasures in heaven)
3. In what ways did Satan deceive Eve by distorting the concept of gain and loss? Scripture Reference: Genesis 3:4-6 (The serpent's deception)

Love as Investment

1. How does human love often function as an investment with expectations of returns? Scripture Reference: Luke 6:35 (Loving without expecting in return)

2. What are some examples of intangible returns we seek when we give love? Scripture Reference: Romans 15:13 (Hope, joy, and peace)
3. How does God's love contrast with the conditional nature of human love as an investment? Scripture Reference: John 3:16 (God's unconditional love)

Let's delve further

1. Lowering Expectations and Limiting Losses:
- The human heart's tendency is to lower expectations to limit losses in love relationships.
- When one invests in a relationship, they expect reciprocation to experience gain.
- Couples often raise each other's expectations through gestures, time, and companionship.
- However, as time progresses, expressions of love may decrease, leading to dissatisfaction.

Key Scripture: Proverbs 13:12 - "Hope deferred makes the heart sick, but a desire fulfilled is a tree of life."

2. The Illusion of Possession and Pride:
- Human love deceives us into believing that we possess love and can produce it.
- In reality, everything we have, including love, belongs to God.
- Thinking love is our possession and creation leads to personal hurt when rejected.
- The pride of considering ourselves self-sufficient and capable hinders genuine love.

Key Scripture: James 1:17 - "Every good gift and every perfect gift is from above, coming down from the Father of lights."

3. Selfish Love and Motivations:
- All human love is fundamentally selfish and motivated by pride.
- Even when we love our loved ones, it stems from selfish desires.
- The core of our hearts is tainted by sin, rendering our righteousness as inadequate.
- Offering our hearts to God, despite their flaws, allows Him to transform us.

Key Scripture: Romans 3:23 - "For all have sinned and fall short of the glory of God."

4. Giving to Receive and Breaking the First Commandment:
- Giving in order to receive positions oneself as a god, assuming the power of creation.
- This violates the first commandment of having no other gods before the Lord.
- Self-centeredness often places our own desires and needs above God's.
- Recognizing this common tendency enables us to realign our priorities.

Key Scripture: Exodus 20:3 - "You shall have no other gods before me."

5. Slavery to Others and the Quest for Control:
- The human heart becomes enslaved to others due to its dependency on their actions.
- Our gains and losses are contingent on what others give, making us vulnerable.
- Attempting to control others through good or bad means stems from lack of trust.
- We are called to trust God rather than seeking control over others.

Key Scripture: Psalm 118:8 - "It is better to take refuge in the Lord than to trust in man."

REFLECTIVE QUESTION

1. How have your own expectations influenced your experiences in love relationships? Have you found that lowering your expectations has limited your losses or led to dissatisfaction?

2. Scriptural Question: In what ways does the concept of possession and pride hinder our ability to love selflessly? How can we align our understanding with the biblical truth that everything we have belongs to God?

3. Personal Reflection: Can you recall a time when you realized that even your acts of love were motivated by selfish desires or pride? How did this realization impact your perspective on your own righteousness and ability to love?

4. Soul-Searching Question: Have you ever caught yourself giving to others with the expectation of receiving something in return? How does this pattern reflect a desire to be in control and play the role of God in relationships?

5. Application Question: How can you cultivate a greater sense of trust in God and relinquish the need to control others in your relationships? What steps can you take to prioritize God's guidance and align your motivations with His love?

6. Personal Experience Sharing: Have you ever felt enslaved to the actions or reactions of others in your relationships? How did this dependency affect your sense of self and well-being?

7. Biblical Reflection: Consider the commandment to have no other gods before the Lord. How can you actively prioritize God in your life and relationships, letting go of the tendency to place yourself or others in the position of ultimate control?

8. Self-Reflection: Take a moment to examine your own heart and motivations in your relationships. How can you seek to cultivate a selfless love that reflects God's love for us?

9. Practical Application: How can you actively demonstrate trust in God and release the need for control in your relationships? Are there specific areas where you can surrender control and rely on God's guidance instead?

10. Encouragement and Prayer: Spend a moment reflecting on God's unconditional love for you and His ability to transform your heart. Pray for His guidance and strength to

overcome the deceptions of love and to cultivate selfless, Christ-like love in your relationships.

As Christians, it is crucial to understand the depths of our hearts and the need for Christ's presence within us.

Main Points:

1. The Deceptive Nature of the Heart (Jeremiah 17:9):
    - The human heart is deceitful above all things and desperately wicked.
    - Just as individuals with alternate realities are convinced of their delusions, our hearts can deceive us into believing falsehoods.
    - We may perceive ourselves as somewhat okay, but the truth is that our hearts are inherently flawed.

2. The Downward Pull of the Heart:
    - The human heart is inclined towards wickedness, akin to a ball rolling downhill.
    - In an upside-down world, our pursuit of greatness can lead us to the depths of wickedness.
    - Our hearts, if left unrestrained, will always gravitate towards the deep end of the wickedness pool.

3. Desperation for Wickedness:
    - The heart's desperation for wickedness is comparable to a person dying of thirst in a desert, willing to brave a cactus patch for water.
    - Our hearts possess an astonishing capacity to be deceived, constantly yearning for wickedness.
    - We must recognize this desperation within us and seek to overcome it with the guidance of Christ.

4. Recognizing Our Blindness:
    - While we can easily identify flaws in others, we often remain blind to our own shortcomings.
    - Jesus highlighted this tendency when He spoke about the speck and plank analogy.
    - We need self-reflection and humility to remove the metaphorical planks from our own eyes before addressing the specks in others'.

Reinforcement and Reflection:
- Reflective Questions:
    1. How can we discern if Christ truly resides in our hearts?

2. In what ways have you observed the deceptive nature of the heart in your own life?
3. How can we avoid being deceived by our hearts and the prevailing wickedness of the world?
4. What steps can we take to cultivate righteousness within our hearts?

- Scriptures to Meditate Upon:
    1. Jeremiah 17:9 - "The heart is deceitful above all things and desperately wicked; who can know it?"
    2. Matthew 7:3-5 - "And why do you look at the speck in your brother's eye, but do not consider the plank in your own eye?"
    3. Mark 8:29 - "He said to them, 'But who do you say that I am?' Peter answered and said to Him, 'You are the Christ.'"

The Deception of Self-Awareness

1. Why is it difficult for us to recognize our own flaws and deception?
2. How does God, through His demonstration, reveal the truth about our hearts?
3. Reflective question: Have you ever experienced a moment of realization regarding the condition of your heart? Describe it and its impact on your life.

The Heart Known Only by God

1. What does Jeremiah 17:10 tell us about God's knowledge of our hearts?
2. How did David, a man after God's own heart, demonstrate an understanding of the hidden motives within his heart?
3. Reflective question: Are you willing to pray David's prayer from Psalm 139:23-24 and allow God to search and reveal your heart to you?

Trials and Revelation

1. How did David's encounter with Bathsheba and Nathan's confrontation reveal the true state of his heart?
2. What did David's subsequent prayer in Psalm 51 reveal about his understanding of the need for a new heart?
3. Reflective question: Have you experienced a trial or confrontation that exposed the hidden sins and desires within your heart? How did it lead you to seek transformation?

The Promise of a New Heart

1. How does Ezekiel 36:26-27 offer hope for those in need of a new heart?
2. What does it mean to receive God's heart and have His Spirit within us?
3. Reflective question: Are you willing to surrender your heart to God, acknowledging your need for His transformational power? Pray and ask Him to give you a new heart.

Key Points:

1. We are often deceived and unable to recognize our own flaws and shortcomings.
2. God, through His demonstration and revelation, shows us the truth about our hearts.
3. Trials and confrontations can bring about a realization of our need for a new heart.
4. God promises to give us a new heart and His Spirit to guide us in His ways.

Scriptures:

- Jeremiah 17:10 - "I, the Lord, search the heart, I test the mind, even to give every man according to his ways, according to the fruit of his doings."
- Psalm 139:23-24 - "Search me, O God, and know my heart; try me, and know my anxieties; and see if there is any wicked way in me, and lead me in the way everlasting."
- 2 Samuel 12:7 - "You are the man!"
- Psalm 51:10-12 - "Create in me a clean heart, O God, and renew a steadfast spirit within me. Do not cast me away from Your presence, and do not take Your Holy Spirit from me. Restore to me the joy of Your salvation, and uphold me by Your generous Spirit."
- Ezekiel 36:26-27 - "I will give you a new heart and put a new spirit within you; I will take the heart of stone out of your flesh and give you a heart of flesh. I will put My Spirit within you and cause you to walk in My statutes, and you will keep My judgments and do them."

NOTE

NOTE

CHAPTER 4:
THE LAW OF LIFE: TAKE TO GIVE

In the book "The Law of Life," we discover a profound principle: the Law of Life is rooted in taking in order to give. This concept is reflected throughout creation, from the growth of a seed to the sacrificial love of Christ. As Christians, we are called to understand and embrace this law, which is deeply connected to our faith. Let us delve into the main points of this teaching, accompanied by relevant scriptures and reflective questions.

Main Points:

1. The Law of Life: Taking to Give

- We must take before we can give. Just as a seed takes from the ground to grow, we too must receive from God before we can give.
- Scripture: John 15:4-5 - "Abide in me, and I in you. As the branch cannot bear fruit by itself, unless it abides in the vine, neither can you, unless you abide in me."

Reflective Question: How can we ensure that we are consistently receiving from God so that we have something to give?

2. The Circuit of Beneficence

- The law of beneficence operates in a continuous cycle of giving. Each part of creation takes and gives to sustain and bless others.
- Scripture: Luke 6:38 - "Give, and it will be given to you. Good measure, pressed down, shaken together, running over, will be put into your lap. For with the measure you use it will be measured back to you."

Reflective Question: How can we actively participate in the circuit of beneficence in our daily lives?

3. The Heart - Divine Love

- God desires to give us a new heart filled with divine love. Unlike human love that expects something in return, divine love gives without expecting personal gain.
- Scripture: Ezekiel 36:26 - "And I will give you a new heart, and a new spirit I will put within you. And I will remove the heart of stone from your flesh and give you a heart of flesh."

Reflective Question: How can we cultivate a heart of divine love that gives without expecting anything in return?

4. Keeping by Giving
   - The principle of keeping by giving teaches us that when we share what we have received from God, we are blessed in return. We find fulfillment and eternal life through self-sacrifice.
   - Scripture: Mark 8:35 - "For whoever would save his life will lose it, but whoever loses his life for my sake and the gospel's will save it."

Reflective Question: In what areas of our lives can we practice self-sacrifice and experience the joy of keeping by giving?

Main Points:

1. Jesus' recognition of His dependence on the Father:
   - Jesus acknowledged that everything He had was from His Father.
   - Scripture: Matthew 5:45, Matthew 8:20.
2. Jesus' humility and surrender to God's will:
   - Jesus understood that He was not His own, but a temple of the Holy Spirit.
   - Our bodies and spirits belong to God, and we should glorify Him.
   - Scripture: 1 Corinthians 6:19-20.
3. Jesus' selflessness and focus on others:
   - Jesus lived, thought, and prayed for others, not for Himself.
   - His concern was for the well-being of those around Him.
   - Scripture: John 8:29.
4. Jesus' ability to endure without personal hurt:
   - By considering others above Himself, Jesus transcended personal hurt.
   - He focused on the impact of others' actions on themselves, not on Himself.
   - Scripture: John 6 (bread of life), Judas' betrayal, Peter's denial.
5. Jesus' limitless love and sacrificial nature:
   - Jesus' love for humanity caused Him to suffer immensely.
   - His capacity to love far surpassed what we can comprehend.
   - Scripture: Various references emphasizing Jesus' selfless acts.

Reflective Questions:

1. How can we imitate Jesus' recognition of our dependence on God in our daily lives?
2. In what ways can we surrender our will to God and align our desires with His?
3. How can we shift our focus from self-centeredness to genuine concern for others?

4. What steps can we take to endure hurt and disappointment without dwelling on personal pain?

5. How can we cultivate a deeper love for others, mirroring Jesus' sacrificial nature?

Main Points and Scriptures:

1. Jesus' Suffering and Love:

- Jesus suffered to bring many sons to glory (Hebrews 2:10).
- His soul was pierced for others when they united in the plots of Satan (The Desire of Ages, p. 752).
- He experienced longing and sympathy in suffering (The Desire of Ages, p. 687).
- Reflective Question: How does understanding Jesus' suffering deepen our appreciation for His love and sacrifice?

2. Reacting in Similar Circumstances:

- Christ's enduring faith and lack of discouragement serve as examples for His followers (The Desire of Ages, p. 679).
- Our reactions should not be influenced by praise or lack of appreciation (In Demonstration of the Spirit, September 4, 1888).
- Having the Spirit of Christ enables us to overlook slights and injuries (Be Gentle unto All Men, May 14, 1895).
- Reflective Question: How can we cultivate a faith that remains steadfast even in challenging situations?

3. Freedom from Self-focus:

- The love of self hinders our peace and causes us to guard against mortification and insult (Thoughts from the Mount of Blessing, p. 16).
- When our life is hidden with Christ in God, neglects and slights do not affect us (Thoughts from the Mount of Blessing, p. 16).
- Trusting in God's vindication allows us to endure with calm patience and trust (Thoughts from the Mount of Blessing, p. 32).
- Reflective Question: How can we shift our focus from self to God, finding peace and strength in His presence?

4. Divine Love - Taking to Give:

- Recognizing ourselves as stewards of God's resources, we must receive from Him first (The Law of Life).
- Love given to others should be a selfless gift, not dependent on personal gain (The Law of Life).

- Our gains and losses are under our control when we trust in God as our faithful Source (The Law of Life).
- Reflective Question: How can we cultivate a heart that seeks to give selflessly, trusting in God's provision?

Conclusion: Embracing the Law of Life, taking to give, is a transformative principle deeply rooted in our Christian faith. Just as God continuously gives, we are called to receive from Him and share His blessings with others. By understanding and applying this law in our lives, we can experience the abundant life God has promised. Let us remember that everything we have is from Him, and through our giving, we reflect His love to the world.

Reflective Question: How can we consistently remind ourselves that everything we have belongs to God and that our giving is a reflection of His love?

Remember to seek God's guidance and discernment as you live out the Law of Life, and may your journey be filled with spiritual growth and blessings

NOTE

NOTE

CHAPTER 5: A DECISIVE TREASURE

In Matthew 6:21, Jesus teaches us about the connection between our treasure and our heart. This study guide explores the concept of treasure, its relationship with the heart, and the decision-making process. By aligning our values with God's Word, we can make choices that honor Him and lead to spiritual growth.

Main Points:

1. The Nature of Treasure:
   - Our treasure is the system by which we determine the value of things in our lives.
   - It helps us decide whether something is a gain or a loss.
   - Our valuation system is a reflection of our heart's priorities (Matthew 6:21).
2. Relative Value and Decision-Making:
   - When faced with choices, we naturally opt for gains over losses.
   - The magnitude of gain or loss is proportional to the value we assign to our treasure.
   - Our valuation system is subjective, influenced by beliefs and convictions.
3. God and True Value:
   - While our perception of value may change, true value is objective and based on God and His Word.
   - Our beliefs shape our evaluation of gains and losses.
   - Understanding God's perspective helps us discern true value.
4. Avoiding Greater Loss:
   - We make choices that avoid greater losses and pursue lesser losses.
   - Our decisions are guided by our beliefs about the potential outcomes.
   - Reflecting on Scripture can illuminate the greater losses we seek to avoid.
5. The Impact of Consequences:
   - To let go of perceived gains, we need to replace them with greater gains or attach them to greater losses.
   - Consequences play a role in shaping our perception of gains and losses.

Scripture References:
1. Matthew 6:21 - "For where your treasure is, there your heart will be also."
2. Malachi 2:16 - "For the Lord God of Israel says that He hates divorce, for it covers one's garment with violence..."
3. Revelation 2:22 - "Indeed I will cast her into a sickbed, and those who commit adultery with her into great tribulation unless they repent of their deeds."

Reflective Questions:
1. What do you consider to be your treasure? How does it impact your decision-making?
2. How does your valuation system align with God's perspective of true value?
3. Can you recall a time when your perception of gain or loss changed based on new understanding from Scripture?
4. How can considering the consequences of your choices help you align with God's desires?
5. In what ways can you cultivate a heart that treasures God above all else?

Other Insights from the book are:

1. Treasuring God above all:
- When we shift our focus from self-centeredness to God-centeredness, He becomes our ultimate treasure.
- Understanding Romans 13:1, we acknowledge that all authorities are appointed by God, prompting us to submit to them.
- Realizing God's constant awareness of our actions, we perceive that disobedience and rebellion against authority are losses directly related to our relationship with Him.

Scripture Reference: Romans 13:1 (NIV) - "Let everyone be subject to the governing authorities, for there is no authority except that which God has established."

Reflective Question: How can we prioritize God as our greatest treasure in a world that often promotes self-centeredness?

2. The insignificance of others' opinions:
- When our treasure is God, the opinions of others hold no weight in influencing our decisions.
- No matter what others may think or say, their perspectives do not impact our choices because they are not our treasure.
- Our decisions should be driven by our devotion to God, not swayed by external influences.

Reflective Question: How can we guard our hearts against being influenced by the opinions of others, staying true to our treasure in God?

3. The choice between self-indulgence and self-denial:
- Naturally, we are inclined to indulge ourselves, considering it a gain.
- However, when we recognize that indulging in sinful pleasures leads to the loss of eternal life and God's favor, self-indulgence becomes a profound loss.
- By valuing the treasures of eternal life, heaven, God's approval, and everlasting relationships, we understand the magnitude of the loss that hell represents.

Scripture Reference: Matthew 16:26 (NIV) - "What good will it be for someone to gain the whole world, yet forfeit their soul?"

Reflective Question: How can we internalize the concept of self-denial as a gain by associating it with the greater treasures of God?

4. The transformational power of God as our treasure:
- When God becomes our supreme treasure, our will aligns with His, and we naturally choose what is pleasing to Him.
- Our hearts adopt God's valuation system, leading us to think, speak, and act in accordance with His will.
- We willingly suffer for the sake of God, seeing it as a lesser loss compared to embracing sin, as suffering upholds and strengthens our relationship with Him.

5. The Heart's Treasure:
- Scripture Reference: 1 John 2:15 ("Do not love the world or the things in the world...")
- When God is our greatest treasure, our hearts are filled with love for Him, and worldly attachments lose their hold on us.
- Reflective Question: What are some areas in your life where you can prioritize God and align with His will?

6. Sin and Self as the Treasure:
- When sin and self become our greatest treasures, we value anything that supports our selfish desires.
- Reflective Question: How can you recognize and address any areas in your life where sin and self have taken precedence over God?

7. The Power of Conviction:
- A change in beliefs may lead to temporary changes in behavior, but conviction brings about permanent transformation.
- Reflective Question: How can you deepen your convictions in God's truth and align your choices with His will?

8. The Seal of Conviction:
- The seal mentioned in Revelation represents a firm conviction based on truth.

- Reflective Question: How can you develop a firm conviction in God's truth that withstands pressure and temptation?

9. Settling into the Truth:
- When God is our treasure, our will aligns with His, leading to obedience and a hatred for sin.
- Reflective Question: How can you cultivate a deep love for God and view sin as the greatest loss?

10. Making God Your Treasure:
- Scripture Reference: Philippians 4:8 ("Finally, brothers and sisters, whatever is true, whatever is noble...")
- Engage in heartfelt reading of God's Word, regular prayer, contemplation of Christ's life, and gratitude for His blessings.
- Reflective Question: How can you prioritize these practices to strengthen your relationship with God?

11. Trusting in God's Promises:
- Scripture Reference: Jeremiah 29:11 ("'For I know the plans I have for you,' declares the Lord...")
- Seek and believe in God's promises, testing them in different circumstances, and allowing the Holy Spirit to work in your heart.
- Reflective Question: How can you actively rely on God's promises in your daily life?

Transformative power of surrendering our lives to God and experiencing His abundant love and grace.

Main Points:

1. The Hidden Treasure and the Pearl of Great Price (Matthew 13:44-46)
    - In these parables, Jesus illustrates the value of the kingdom of heaven.
    - Just as a man sells all he has to possess the treasure or the pearl, we must be willing to surrender everything for the sake of embracing God's kingdom.
    - The Holy Spirit plays a vital role in revealing the preciousness of the goodly pearl.

2. Seeking the Treasure: A Personal Testimony
    - The author shares their lifelong pursuit of the hidden treasure.
    - Various methods were employed, such as attending church, engaging in prayer, studying the Bible, and serving others.
    - However, true understanding of the treasure remained elusive until a pivotal moment.

3. Surrendering to God's Control
   - The author recounts a period of darkness and desperation when they realized their inability to break free from bondage.
   - God calls for complete surrender and control over every aspect of our lives.
   - The initial reluctance to trust God completely is overcome by recognizing the destructive nature of self-reliance.

4. The Wheelbarrow of Faith
   - An analogy of a tightrope artist and a wheelbarrow illustrates the need for unwavering faith and surrender.
   - Getting into the wheelbarrow symbolizes complete trust in God's ability to guide and protect us.
   - Surrendering control leads to a new life characterized by liberation, joy, and victory.

5. Transformation through Prayer and Study
   - Consistency in prayer and study of God's word, which facilitate profound changes, are the result of the complete surrender of "getting into the wheelbarrow."
   - The author's journey towards consistency in prayer, learning about God's love, and teaching others underscores the transformative power of spiritual disciplines in the context of complete surrender.
   - Reflective questions: Have you tried to be consistent in prayer and study of God's word without complete surrender? If so, how successful were you at being consistent? In the context of complete surrender, how has consistent prayer and study impacted your relationship with God? How has it transformed your perspective on His love and mercy?

6. Belief in the Infinite God
   - Contemplating the vastness of the universe and God's love for humanity deepens our belief.
   - Recognizing the magnitude of Jesus' sacrifice highlights the immeasurable value of the gift of salvation.
   - Reflective question: How does contemplating God's love for you impact your understanding of your worth and significance?

Reiteration: You will never accept Jesus as your hidden treasure and pearl of great price unless you first accept that you are His hidden treasure and pearl of great price. Embracing the hidden treasure and the pearl of great price represents our wholehearted surrender to God. By relinquishing control and trusting in His guidance, we experience profound transformation, joy, and victory. Let us continually seek the preciousness of Jesus, embrace

His love, and grow in our faith through consistent prayer, study, and reflection on His infinite love and sacrifice.

Scripture References:

- Matthew 13:44-46
- Matthew 19:21
- Matthew 11:28-30, Luke 9:23
- John 3:16
- Jeremiah 17:9
- Romans 7:15-24, 6:23, 6:16
- Proverbs 24:16
- John 6:39
- Ephesians 3:17-19
- Mark 9:24
- Psalm 89:8
- Matthew 5:45
- 1 John 1:9
- Psalm 9:1

Scripture Reference: Philippians 3:8 (NIV) - "What is more, I consider everything a loss because of the surpassing worth of knowing Christ Jesus my Lord, for whose sake I have lost all things."

Reflective Question: How can we continually prioritize God as our treasure, allowing His transformational power to guide our choices and embrace suffering for His sake?

Key Points:

1. The overwhelming gift of Jesus: Reflecting on the priceless sacrifice of Jesus, we realize His infinite value and the depth of God's love for us (Romans 5:8).

2. The revelation of God's glory: Similar to Moses' encounter with God, we experience the revealing of God's glory in our lives, to the extent we can handle (Exodus 33:18-23).

3. The gift of belief: Recognizing that belief in Jesus changes everything, we understand the immense importance of faith and how it shapes our perception of His preciousness.

4. The pain of rejection: Contemplating Jesus' sacrifice, we empathize with the heartache He experienced for others when His love was rejected by the ones He came to save (John 6:66).

5. Confronting the weight of sin: Realizing the harm caused by sin and the separation it creates from God's plans for our lives, we develop a deep aversion to it (Psalm 17:3).

6. The surpassing worth of Jesus: Comparing the allure of sin to the immeasurable value of Jesus, we understand that nothing can compare to His worth (Philippians 3:7,8).

7. Freedom from sin's attraction: Embracing the true value of Jesus, sin loses its power to tempt and attract us, leading us to obedience and delighting in God's will (Psalm 40:8).
8. Perfect peace in Jesus: Recognizing that even in the face of loss and challenges, having Jesus as our treasure provides us with unshakable peace and abundant joy (Romans 15:13).
9. Sharing in Jesus' experience: Through faith, we can experience the same victory over sin, peace, and joy that Jesus experienced during His earthly life.
10. The longing for more: Expressing a desire for continued revelations of God's love, we seek a deeper and more consistent experience of His presence (Exodus 34:29-35).

Reflective Questions:

1. How does contemplating the sacrifice of Jesus make you feel about the depth of God's love for you?
2. Have you ever experienced a revelation of God's glory in your life? How did it impact your faith?
3. In what ways have you personally rejected or embraced the love of Jesus?
4. How does recognizing the infinite value of Jesus transform your perception of sin?
5. What worldly desires or attractions lose their appeal when compared to the surpassing worth of Jesus?
6. Can you recall a time when you felt liberated from the power of sin? How did it affect your obedience to God?
7. How does the presence of Jesus bring you peace and joy, regardless of life's circumstances?
8. Are there areas in your life where you still struggle to see Jesus as your ultimate treasure?
9. What steps can you take to deepen your relationship with Jesus and experience more of His love and presence?
10. How can you share the transformative power of Jesus' love with others?

Scripture References:

- Romans 5:8
- Exodus 33:18-23
- John 6:66
- Psalm 17:3
- Philippians 3:7,8
- Psalm 40:8
- Romans

NOTE

NOTE

CHAPTER 6: LEAVING YOUR BAGGAGE BEHIND

The past can often determine the direction of our lives, and unfortunately, it tends to lead us astray. But there is hope—freedom from the baggage we have carried for years. The solution lies at the cross, where Jesus, the unwearied servant of humanity, became our sin so that we might become the righteousness of God in Him. Let us delve deeper into this profound truth and understand how it impacts our lives as Christians.

Main Points:

1. The Sacrificial Love of Jesus

    Scripture Reference: 2 Corinthians 5:21

    Reiteration: Jesus, the spotless Son of God, willingly bore our sin and became sin itself on the cross. Through His selfless sacrifice, He offers us the opportunity to become the righteousness of God in Him.

    Reflective Question: How does Jesus' sacrificial love inspire us to let go of our past and embrace His righteousness?

2. The Incomprehensible Exchange

    Reiteration: Jesus, who was sinless, took upon Himself the sin that separates us from God. In turn, He offers us His righteousness.

    Reflective Question: How does it feel to know that Jesus willingly took on our sin so that we could receive His righteousness? How can this truth impact our lives today?

3. Christ's Perfect Life

    Reiteration: Before the cross, Jesus lived a perfect life—fully God and fully man. He responded to every situation with love, selflessness, and perfect obedience to God.

    Reflective Question: How can we enter into the perfect example of Christ's selflessness and obedience?

4. Our Imperfect Lives

    Reiteration: Unlike Christ, we fall short and carry the burden of sin and its consequences. We often take things personally, respond poorly to others, and struggle to overcome temptation.

    Reflective Question: How does acknowledging our own imperfections and weaknesses help us seek the transformative power of the cross in our lives?

5. The Weight of Baggage

    Reiteration: Our past mistakes and negative influences create ripples that affect not only us but also those around us. Our baggage becomes heavy and burdensome, leading to the penalty of death.

    Reflective Question: How has your past influenced your present circumstances and relationships? How can surrendering that baggage to the cross bring healing and restoration?

The Sanctuary Service

The Purpose of the Sanctuary Service

1. What was the purpose of the sanctuary service in the Old Testament?
2. How did the sacrificial system work in transferring sin from the sinner to the sanctuary?
3. Why did the sin transfer require the shedding of blood?
4. Reflect on the significance of confessing one's sins before laying hands on the sacrificial animal.

The Day of Atonement

1. What transpired during the annual Day of Atonement ceremony?
2. Describe the symbolism behind the Lord's goat and the scapegoat.
3. How did the high priest's actions with the blood on the mercy seat signify God's plan for sin?
4. Reflect on the scapegoat's fate in the desert and its implications for our own sins.

Jesus, Our High Priest

1. How does Jesus fulfill the role of the sacrificial Lamb of God?
2. What happened to Jesus from the last supper until His death on the cross?
3. How does Jesus, as our High Priest, continue to intercede for us in the heavenly sanctuary?
4. Reflect on the profound truth that Jesus bore our sins and paid their penalty through His sacrifice.

God's Ultimate Plan for Sin

1. What is God's ultimate plan to deal with sin?
2. How does our confession of sins today align with the transfer of sins in the sanctuary service?
3. Reflect on the anticipation of the day when Satan will bear the accumulated sins he instigated others to commit and be destroyed along with sin itself.

4. How does understanding God's plan for sin inspire hope and freedom in our lives?

Key Points:

1. The sanctuary service of the Old Testament revealed God's plan for dealing with sin.
2. The sacrificial system involved the transfer of sin from the sinner to the sanctuary through the shedding of blood.
3. The Day of Atonement symbolized the ultimate fulfillment of God's plan through Jesus, our High Priest.
4. Jesus bore our sins on the cross and continues to intercede for us in the heavenly sanctuary.
5. God's ultimate plan is to destroy sin along with Satan, ensuring our eternal freedom.

Scripture References:

- Leviticus 16:30 - "For on this day shall atonement be made for you to cleanse you. You shall be clean before the Lord from all your sins."
- Hebrews 9:22 - "Indeed, under the law almost everything is purified with blood, and without the shedding of blood there is no forgiveness of sins."
- 1 Peter 2:24 - "He himself bore our sins in his body on the tree, that we might die to sin and live to righteousness. By his wounds you have been healed."
- Revelation 20:10 - "And the devil who had deceived them was thrown into the lake of fire and sulfur where the beast and the false prophet were, and they will be tormented day and night forever and ever."

Reflective Questions:

1. How does the understanding of God's plan for sin impact your view of forgiveness and redemption?
2. Reflect on the freedom you experience when you truly lay your sins at the foot of the cross.
3. How does the knowledge of Jesus' intercession for you as the High Priest bring comfort and assurance?
4. Consider the significance of sin being ultimately destroyed. How does this inspire you to live a holy and victorious life?

At/After the Cross

The concept of leaving our baggage behind is deeply rooted in the profound sacrifice of Jesus Christ on the cross. He willingly took upon Himself the burden of our sins, our past mistakes, and the consequences of our actions. Through His selfless act, He offers us a divine exchange—a transformative journey where we can experience forgiveness, freedom, and a new life in Him.

Main Points:

1. The Cross: Jesus Takes Our Place

- Jesus took responsibility for our sins and selfishness, bearing the consequences we deserved.
- He suffered the penalty as both the perpetrator and the victim, carrying the weight of our past.
- Through His sacrificial death, Jesus offers to carry our baggage and sets us free.

Scripture: Isaiah 53:5 (NIV) - "But he was pierced for our transgressions, he was crushed for our iniquities; the punishment that brought us peace was on him, and by his wounds, we are healed."

2. The Divine Exchange: Placed in the Gun Barrel of His Life

- As Jesus takes our place, He invites us into the timeline of His life.
- In this exchange, we receive eternal life and the blessings of His perfect life.
- His life becomes a guiding force, empowering us to overcome temptation and negative responses.

Scripture: 2 Corinthians 5:21 (NIV) - "God made him who had no sin to be sin for us so that in him we might become the righteousness of God."

3. The Transformative Power of Faith and Grace

- Faith is necessary to receive the gift of grace, accepting the divine exchange as our own.
- Believing in Jesus and His sacrificial love grants us everlasting life.
- Through faith, we become recipients of Jesus' perfect record and experience freedom from guilt and fear.

Scripture: Ephesians 2:8-9 (NIV) - "For it is by grace you have been saved, through faith—and this is not from yourselves, it is the gift of God—not by works, so that no one can boast."

Reflective Questions:

1. How does understanding the divine exchange impact your view of Jesus' sacrifice on the cross?
2. In what areas of your life do you struggle to let go of past mistakes and negative responses?
3. How can faith and trust in God's grace bring freedom from guilt and fear?

4. Reflect on a specific instance where you can apply the concept of leaving your baggage behind. What steps can you take to embrace the divine exchange in that situation?

Applying scriptural principles to let go of hurt, bitterness, and victimhood.

I. The Weight of Emotional Baggage

1. Reiteration: When we hold onto the hurts caused by others, our hearts become burdened with emotional baggage.
2. Reflective Question: How has holding onto past hurts affected your emotional well-being and relationships?
3. Biblical Perspective:
    - Scripture: Ephesians 4:31-32 (NIV) - "Get rid of all bitterness, rage and anger, brawling and slander, along with every form of malice. Be kind and compassionate to one another, forgiving each other, just as in Christ God forgave you."
    - Reflection: God calls us to release our bitterness and anger through forgiveness, mirroring His own forgiveness toward us.

II. Love Beyond Personal Offense

1. Reiteration: It is easier to love those who hurt others when we are not directly affected by their actions.
2. Reflective Question: How does personal involvement in a hurtful situation impact your ability to extend love and forgiveness?
3. Biblical Perspective:
    - Scripture: Matthew 5:44 (NIV) - "But I tell you, love your enemies and pray for those who persecute you."
    - Reflection: Jesus teaches us to love and pray for our enemies, transcending personal offense and embracing a higher love rooted in His example.

III. Finding Freedom Through the Cross

1. Reiteration: The cross of Jesus offers us liberation from our past and the negative emotions associated with victimhood.
2. Reflective Question: In what ways have you experienced the freedom and healing that comes from surrendering your pain to Jesus?
3. Biblical Perspective:
    - Scripture: Galatians 2:20 (NIV) - "I have been crucified with Christ and I no longer live, but Christ lives in me. The life I now live in the body, I live by faith in the Son of God, who loved me and gave himself for me."

- Reflection: Through the cross, we can exchange our victimhood for the life of Christ within us, allowing His love and forgiveness to flow through us.

IV. Accepting the Divine Exchange and Letting Go

1. Reiteration: Coming to the cross requires letting go of guilt and accepting the divine exchange offered by God's grace.
2. Reflective Question: Are there areas in your life where you struggle to fully accept God's forgiveness and release guilt and shame?
3. Biblical Perspective:
   - Scripture: 1 John 1:9 (NIV) - "If we confess our sins, he is faithful and just and will forgive us our sins and purify us from all unrighteousness."
   - Reflection: Confessing our sins and accepting God's forgiveness frees us from guilt, allowing us to embrace a life of righteousness and transformation.

Let us embark on this journey of healing and freedom.

Key Points:

1. The Plan of Salvation:
- God's plan of salvation was established before we even recognized our need for it.
- Jesus, the Lamb slain from the foundation of the world, came to seek and save the lost.
- God's love was demonstrated when Christ died for us while we were still sinners (Revelation 13:8, Luke 19:10, Romans 5:8).
2. Working of the Holy Spirit:
- The Holy Spirit takes the initiative in our lives, stirring a desire for forgiveness, restoration, and righteousness.
- Our natural inclination is toward sin, but God's Spirit works within us, shaping our hearts and minds (Romans 8:7, Philippians 2:13).
3. Conviction of Sin:
- Through the Holy Spirit's work, we become aware of God's law and recognize our own sinful nature.
- The law reveals our shortcomings, leading to conviction of our need for a Savior (1 John 3:4, Romans 3:20, Psalm 51:3).
4. Cooperation of the Will:
- Once convicted, we must engage our will to choose whom we will serve.
- Surrendering our desires and choosing God's will is essential in the decision-making process (Joshua 24:15).

5. Choose to Fulfill the Conditions of Forgiveness:
   - Confession, repentance, and restoration are necessary steps in seeking forgiveness.
   - Confession involves acknowledging the wrong without offering excuses, seeking forgiveness, and making proper restitution (1 John 1:9).

Reflective Question: Are there any unresolved issues in your life that require confession, repentance, or restoration?

6. Believe & Accept the Divine Exchange at the Cross:
   - Through faith, we accept the divine exchange at the cross, where Jesus paid the price for our sins.
   - By complying with the conditions of forgiveness, we experience the peace and joy that come from being forgiven (John 3:16).

Reflective Question: How does accepting God's forgiveness and embracing the divine exchange bring freedom to your life?

Results of Forgiveness:
- No more guilt: Through forgiveness, we are freed from the burden of guilt, even though we remember our past actions.
- No more bitterness: Forgiveness releases us from bitterness as we recognize that others' actions are no longer against us, but against Jesus.
- Love and compassion: God's love compels us to love others and desire their freedom and restoration.
- Assisting in others' freedom: Cooperation with the Holy Spirit enables us to assist others on their journey of forgiveness and healing.

Reflective Question: How does forgiveness impact your relationships and your ability to show love and compassion?

Taking Up Our Cross:
- Taking up our cross means denying ourselves, following Jesus, and obeying God at any cost.
- It involves imitating Christ, being willing to suffer and obeying His commandments (Mark 8:34, Matthew 5:23-24).

Reflective Question: What does taking up your cross look like in your daily life? How can you imitate Christ in your thoughts, words, and actions?

NOTE

NOTE

CHAPTER 7:
THE TALENT OF SUFFERING

Loss and suffering are inevitable parts of life, but as Christians, we can find solace and guidance in the Word of God. This study guide explores the concept of "The Talent of Suffering" based on the book "The Law of Life." By delving into the teachings of Job, Paul, and other biblical references, we will gain insights into how to cope with the loss of loved ones and find strength in the midst of hardships.

1. Understanding Loss:
- At birth, we possess nothing, and at death, we take nothing with us.
- Our journey between birth and death is filled with joys, sorrows, and encounters with people.
- Job's perspective: Acknowledging that we enter and exit the world empty-handed, anything we have during our lifetime is a gain (Job 1:21).

Reflective Question: How does the realization that we are temporary stewards rather than owners of worldly possessions change our perspective on loss?

2. Gaining Perspective:
- Embracing the role of stewards: Recognizing that everything belongs to God, and we are merely caretakers.
- A case of mourning a child's death: Focusing on what was gained during the child's life rather than mourning the failure of future expectations.
- Shifting from loss to gratitude: Acknowledging the blessings and experiences shared with loved ones during their presence.

Reflective Question: How can shifting our perspective from loss to gratitude impact our emotional well-being and outlook on life's challenges?

3. The Power of God's Providence:
- Paul's assurance: All things work together for good for those who love God and are called according to His purpose (Romans 8:28).
- God's presence and protection: His encompassing love shields His children from evil.
- Endurance through God's strength: Trusting that God will never allow us to face challenges beyond what we can bear, providing a way of escape (1 Corinthians 10:13).

Reflective Question: How does knowing that God works everything for our good and provides strength in our trials give us hope and resilience?

4. Suffering as a Talent:

- Suffering as an endowed ability: Just as talents are gifts for God's glory, suffering can be utilized to bring glory to God.

- Comfort through shared experiences: Those who have triumphed over similar adversities can offer the most profound comfort.

- Becoming instruments of salvation: God weaves His love and goodness through our suffering, allowing us to minister to others.

Reflective Question: In what ways can our personal experiences of suffering become instruments for comforting and guiding others?

Suffering, as strange as it may sound, can be considered a talent in the eyes of God. Satan, the enemy of God, seeks to inflict pain upon His children, knowing that it hurts God deeply. But God, in His infinite wisdom, desires to reach out to His suffering children and bring them comfort. However, He requires human agents who have experienced and overcome suffering themselves to effectively reach out and provide solace to those in need. This study guide delves into the concept of suffering as a talent, emphasizing its significance from a biblical perspective.

Main Points:

1. God's Plan and Human Agency:

- God, in His great plan for redeeming humanity, delegated to human agents the privilege of extend His helping hand to those in need.

- Cooperation with God's plan involves actively seeking opportunities to assist and comfort others. Scripture reference: John 10:10.

2. The Purpose of Suffering:

- By going through our own suffering and emerging with God's deliverance, we gain the ability to understand and empathize with others who are currently suffering.

- Our suffering becomes a testimony of God's faithfulness, enabling us to offer hope and guidance to those enduring similar trials.

- Burying our talent of suffering hinders God's purpose and prevents His love from reaching His suffering children.

- Scripture reference: Philippians 1:29.

3. Instruments in God's Hands:

- God, the master surgeon, utilizes human beings as instruments to reach and heal others.

- The more we have suffered, the more effectively we can identify with and help those experiencing similar trials.

- Scripture reference: The Desire of Ages, p. 224.

4. Suffering as a Refining Process:
   - Suffering plays a vital role in molding our character and shaping us into the image of Christ.
   - Just as pressure and heat transform coal into a precious diamond, suffering refines us into valuable vessels that reflect God's love and character.
   - Trials and obstacles are God's chosen means of discipline and conditions for spiritual growth.
   - Scripture reference: This Day With God, p. 427.
5. Yielding to the Master Worker:
   - Like clay in the hands of a potter, we must surrender ourselves to God's molding and shaping.
   - God refines us through various experiences, kneading, working, and perfecting us according to His will.
   - Our role is to yield to His transformative work, allowing Him to fashion us into vessels fit for His service.
   - Scripture reference: The Ministry of Healing, pp. 469-471.

Reflective Questions:
1. How has your personal experience of suffering enabled you to connect with and comfort others in similar situations?
2. In what ways can you actively cooperate with God's plan to reach out and assist those who are suffering?
3. How does the perspective of suffering as a refining process impact your understanding of its purpose in your life?
4. Are there any specific Scriptures that have provided comfort or guidance during your own journey of suffering?

WHO CAN HURT ME

Finding hope and healing even in the midst of difficult circumstances.

Key Points:
1. The Source of Hurt:
   - From an emotional and spiritual standpoint, no one has the power to hurt us. We have the ultimate control over our thoughts and reactions.
   - Our breathing, eating, drinking, and thinking directly impact our physical and emotional well-being.

- Scripture Reference: Proverbs 23:7a - "For as he thinks in his heart, so is he."

2. The Case of Martha:
- Martha's health declined rapidly after discovering her husband's infidelity, despite the fact that he had been unfaithful throughout their entire marriage.
- It was Martha's thinking and perception of personal loss, not her husband's actions, that contributed to her decline.
- By choosing gratitude for the support and good times they shared, Martha could have experienced better health outcomes.
- Scripture Reference: Philippians 4:8 - "Finally, brothers and sisters, whatever is true, whatever is noble, whatever is right, whatever is pure, whatever is lovely, whatever is admirable—if anything is excellent or praiseworthy—think about such things."

3. Taking Personal Offenses:
- Often, we take things personally and attribute the hurtful actions or words of others as a reflection of ourselves.
- Just as spilled liquid reveals what was in the cup, people's hurtful words or actions stem from what is already in their hearts.
- Understanding this truth frees us from taking offense personally and allows us to extend grace and forgiveness.
- Scripture Reference: Luke 6:45 - "The good person out of the good treasure of his heart produces good, and the evil person out of his evil treasure produces evil, for out of the abundance of the heart his mouth speaks."

Reflective Questions:
1. How does the understanding that no one can hurt you emotionally or spiritually empower you to take control of your thoughts and reactions?
2. Reflect on a personal hurt you have experienced. How did your thinking about the situation contribute to your emotional well-being?
3. In what ways have you taken offense personally? How can you shift your perspective to recognize that others' actions are a reflection of their own hearts?
4. What steps can you take to guard your heart and fill it with thoughts that align with God's truth and love?
5. How does recognizing that your response to circumstances reveals what is truly in your heart motivate you to pursue inner healing and transformation?

Margaret's Journey

Margaret, plagued by a chronic cough and urinary incontinence, discovered that the root cause of her physical ailments was an ongoing conflict with her daughter. By understanding the Law of Life and embracing God's love, Margaret learned to let go of control and replace negative thoughts with positive ones. Reflecting on this story, we are reminded of the biblical truth that forgiveness and love have the power to heal (Matthew 6:14-15, Colossians 3:13).

Reflective Questions:

1. How can we apply the Law of Life in our relationships, particularly in moments of conflict?
2. How does forgiveness contribute to emotional and physical healing, as illustrated by Margaret's story?
3. In what ways can we cultivate positive thoughts and attitudes towards others, even in challenging situations?

Janet's Transformation

Janet's debilitating migraines, recurring every weekend, were traced back to her deep-seated hatred for her alcoholic father. Through the Law of Life, Janet embarked on a journey of forgiveness, seeing her father through God's eyes of love. As she replaced negative thoughts with positive ones, her migraines ceased. This story aligns with biblical teachings on forgiveness and the power of love (Ephesians 4:31-32, 1 John 4:7-8).

Reflective Questions:

1. How does harboring resentment and unforgiveness impact our emotional and physical well-being?
2. What steps can we take to release negative emotions and replace them with love and forgiveness?
3. How can we see others through God's eyes of love, even in challenging circumstances?

Carl's Struggle

Carl, a diabetic rancher, faced a series of amputations and uncontrolled blood sugar levels despite medical interventions. It was only when his physician addressed his overwhelming guilt through prayer and forgiveness that Carl experienced healing. This story highlights the significance of releasing guilt and accepting God's forgiveness (1 John 1:9, Psalm 103:12).

Reflective Questions:

1. How does guilt and self-condemnation affect our physical health and well-being?
2. In what ways can prayer and seeking God's forgiveness contribute to healing and restoration?
3. How can we let go of guilt and embrace God's grace and forgiveness in our lives?

The Power of Forgiveness
1. What were the lifestyle issues Michelle faced when she came to the lifestyle center?
2. How did Michelle's relationship with her mother affect her battle with cancer?
3. What role did forgiveness play in Michelle's healing journey?
4. Reflective Question: Are there any unresolved conflicts or resentments in your life that may be affecting your physical or emotional well-being?

Chapter 2: God as the Ultimate Source
1. How did Michelle's perception of her mother as her source contribute to her suffering?
2. What biblical principles can we apply to understand God as our ultimate source of love and healing?
3. Reflective Question: Do you struggle with relying on God as your source, or do you find yourself seeking validation from other people or worldly things?

Chapter 3: The Mind-Body Connection
1. What did Michelle's experience teach us about the foundation of diseases in the mind?
2. How does the state of our minds and emotions impact our physical health?
3. Reflective Question: Are there any negative thought patterns or emotions that you need to address in order to experience healing and wholeness?

Chapter 4: Healing and Restoration
1. What was the relationship between Michelle's mindset and her cancer markers?
2. How did Michelle's renewed perspective lead to improved health outcomes?
3. Reflective Question: How can you apply the principles of forgiveness, relying on God as your source, and renewing your mind to experience healing and restoration in your own life?

Key Points:
1. Forgiveness and resolving conflicts are crucial for physical and emotional healing.
2. Recognizing God as our ultimate source of love, strength, and healing brings perspective and peace.
3. The mind-body connection plays a significant role in disease prevention and recovery.
4. Healing and restoration are possible when we align our thoughts, emotions, and beliefs with biblical truths and principles.

Scriptures:
1. Matthew 6:14-15 - "For if you forgive other people when they sin against you, your heavenly Father will also forgive you. But if you do not forgive others their sins, your Father will not forgive your sins."

2. Psalm 46:1 - "God is our refuge and strength, an ever-present help in trouble."
3. Romans 12:2 - "Do not conform to the pattern of this world, but be transformed by the renewing of your mind. Then you will be able to test and approve what God's will is—his good, pleasing and perfect will."
4. Isaiah 53:5 - "But he was pierced for our transgressions, he was crushed for our iniquities; the punishment that brought us peace was on him, and by his wounds, we are healed."

Reflective Questions:

1. How can you practice forgiveness in your relationships to experience greater emotional and physical well-being?
2. How can you deepen your reliance on God as your ultimate source of love, strength, and healing?
3. What steps can you take to renew your mind and align your thoughts with God's truth for improved health and wholeness?

NOTE

NOTE

CHAPTER 8:
THE LAW OF LOVE...AND HEALTH

The following study guide is based on the book "The Law of Life" and focuses on understanding the profound connection between love, health, and biblical principles. It explores the concept of love relationships and their impact on our physical and spiritual well-being. By delving into the teachings of God's law and reflecting on its application in our lives, we can uncover the keys to experiencing love, health, and harmony as Christians.

I. Love Relationships and God's Design

- Two legitimate love relationships: Taking and giving
- God's original plan: Taking from Him as the only source, giving to others
- The enemy's deception: Reversing the equation and giving to take
- The consequences: Human love and its detrimental effects

Reiterating the Main Points:

- God designed us to take from Him and give to others.
- The "new order" of things, influenced by sin, leads to death.
- Human love often follows the enemy's plan, leading to negative outcomes.

Scripture References:

- 1 John 4:19: "We love because he first loved us."
- Romans 5:8: "But God demonstrates his own love for us in this: While we were still sinners, Christ died for us."

Reflective Questions:

1. How has the enemy deceived us into giving to take rather than taking from God to give?
2. In what ways can you identify the negative effects of human love in your life?

II. The Commandments and Love Relationships

- The two tables of stone and their purpose
- Exclusive and inclusive commands of the Ten Commandments
- Exclusive commands: Taking from God as the only source
- Inclusive commands: Giving love to others unconditionally

Reiterating the Main Points:
- The first four commandments govern the exclusive love relationship with God.
- The last six commandments guide the inclusive love relationship of giving to others.
- Honoring parents is an inclusive commandment, regardless of their qualities.

Scripture References:
- Exodus 20:3-17: The Ten Commandments
- Matthew 22:37-40: Jesus' summary of the commandments

Reflective Questions:
1. How can you apply the inclusive commands of honoring parents and giving love to others in your daily life?
2. Are there any exclusive love relationships that hinder your connection with God?

III. Dependency and Independence in Love Relationships
- Understanding dependency and independence in the context of love
- The analogy of the mountain stream and farms
- Dependency on the wrong sources leads to frustration, control, and hurt
- The restoration of divine love through God's work in our hearts

Reiterating the Main Points:
- Dependency on sources we take from leads to frustration and control.
- Giving love to others makes us independent of their influence.
- God's work in our hearts restores the original divine love relationship.

Scripture References:
- Psalm 62:5: "Yes, my soul, find rest in God; my hope comes from him."
- Galatians 5:1: "It is for freedom that Christ has set us free."

Reflective Questions:
1. Reflect on the sources you are dependent on. Are they hindering your relationship with God?
2. How can you cultivate independence in your love relationships while still showing God's love?

IV. The Law, Sin, and Health
- The law as a governing force in our lives
- Sin as the root cause of disease
- The importance of obeying God's commandments for health

- Healing through surrender, faith, and compliance with God's conditions

Reiterating the Main Points:

- The law governs our lives and guides us towards health. -.
- Sin, disobedience, and breaking the law lead to physical and spiritual sickness.
- Obedience to God's commandments is essential for experiencing health and wholeness.
- Healing comes through surrendering to God, having faith, and complying with His conditions.

Scripture References:

- Exodus 15:26: "If you listen carefully to the LORD your God and do what is right in his eyes, if you pay attention to his commands and keep all his decrees, I will not bring on you any of the diseases I brought on the Egyptians, for I am the LORD, who heals you."
- James 5:14-15: "Is anyone among you sick? Let them call the elders of the church to pray over them and anoint them with oil in the name of the Lord. And the prayer offered in faith will make the sick person well; the Lord will raise them up. If they have sinned, they will be forgiven."

Reflective Questions:

1. In what areas of your life do you struggle with disobedience to God's commandments?
2. How can you access obedience to God's law and integrate it into your lifestyle for improved health?

V. Love, Forgiveness, and Emotional Healing

- Love as the foundation of forgiveness and emotional healing
- Unforgiveness as a barrier to experiencing love and health
- The power of forgiveness in releasing emotional burdens and promoting well-being
- Seeking God's forgiveness and extending it to others for restoration

Reiterating the Main Points:

- Love serves as the basis for forgiveness and emotional healing.
- Unforgiveness hinders the flow of love and adversely affects our health.
- Forgiveness has the power to release emotional burdens and promote well-being.

Scripture References:

- Ephesians 4:32: "Be kind and compassionate to one another, forgiving each other, just as in Christ God forgave you."
- Matthew 6:14-15: "For if you forgive other people when they sin against you, your heavenly Father will also forgive you. But if you do not forgive others their sins, your Father will not forgive your sins."

Reflective Questions:
1. Is there anyone in your life whom you need to forgive in order to experience emotional healing and improved health?
2. How can you extend God's forgiveness to others, even when it seems challenging?

VI. Love, Service, and Physical Healing
- Love expressed through service as a catalyst for physical healing
- The example of Jesus' ministry of love and healing
- Serving others as an act of love and a means of experiencing God's healing power
- The connection between love, joy, and physical well-being

Reiterating the Main Points:
- Serving others in love has a positive impact on physical healing.
- Jesus' ministry demonstrates the power of love in healing the sick.
- Love-driven service opens the door for experiencing God's healing power.

Scripture References:
- Mark 10:45: "For even the Son of Man did not come to be served, but to serve, and to give his life as a ransom for many."
- Proverbs 17:22: "A cheerful heart is good medicine, but a crushed spirit dries up the bones."

Reflective Questions:
1. How can you incorporate acts of service into your life as an expression of love?
2. Have you experienced the healing power of joy and love in your physical well-being?

VII. Living a Life of Love and Health
- The call to live a life of love and health as followers of Christ
- Cultivating a daily relationship with God to experience His love and guidance
- Practicing obedience, forgiveness, and service for a healthy and fulfilling life
- Trusting in God's provision for physical, emotional, and spiritual well-being

Reiterating the Main Points:
- Followers of Christ are called to live a life of love and health.
- Nurturing a daily relationship with God is essential for experiencing His love and guidance.
- Practicing obedience, forgiveness, and service leads to a healthy and fulfilling life.
- Trusting in God's provision encompasses all aspects of well-being.

Scripture References:

- 1 Corinthians 16:14: "Do everything in love."
- Proverbs 3:5-6: "Trust in the LORD with all your heart and lean not on your own understanding; in all your ways submit to him, and he will make your paths straight."

Reflective Questions:

1. How can you make love a central focus in every aspect of your life?
2. What steps can you take to deepen your relationship with God and experience His love and guidance?

As you engage with these reflective questions, prayerfully consider how you can apply these principles to your life. Remember, God desires your holistic well-being and invites you to walk in His love and experience the abundant life He offers.

May God bless you abundantly as you seek to align your life with His loving and health-giving principles.

NOTE

NOTE

CHAPTER 9: ENEMY WARFARE

In 1 Peter 5:8, we are warned to be vigilant and sober-minded because our adversary, the devil, seeks to devour us like a roaring lion. As Christians, we need to be aware that there is an enemy who desires to destroy us and hinder our relationship with God. The story of Job serves as a powerful illustration of this spiritual battle. Let us delve into the depths of this topic and explore the biblical truths surrounding enemy warfare.

Main Points:

1. The Controversy between God and Satan:

- The word "Satan" means accuser, and he constantly brings false accusations against God and His people.
- Rather than engaging in an argument, God allows Satan to put his accusations to the test, proving him wrong without entering into a debate.
- Accusing others is not God's character, and as followers of Christ, we should refrain from accusing and condemning others.

Scripture Reference: Luke 3:14, John 8:11, John 5:45, Mark 15:3, 2 Peter 2:11, Jude 1:9

Reflective Question: How can we emulate God's character of love and refrain from accusing others?

2. God's Limits on Satan's Power:

- God sets limits on Satan's ability to harm believers. Satan can only operate within the boundaries allowed by God.
- The story of Job reveals that Satan was permitted to afflict him but was not given the authority to take his life.
- Not all afflictions are caused by Satan; sometimes, people give him permission to exert control through their choices and actions.

Scripture Reference: Job 1:12, Job 2:6, Matthew 9:32-33, Matthew 12:22, Matthew 17:14-18

Reflective Question: How can we discern when afflictions are a result of our choices or spiritual warfare, and how can we seek God's protection?

3. Giving Satan Permission:

- Satan can gain access and influence in our lives when we have unconfessed sins or unresolved issues.

- Specific confession and repentance close the doors through which the enemy gains access.
- Personal stories demonstrate how confessing past sins and seeking God's intervention can bring immediate transformation.

Reflective Question: Are there any unconfessed sins or unresolved issues in our lives that may be giving the enemy access? How can we actively seek God's intervention?

Reiteration: In our journey as Christians, we must remember that we have an enemy seeking to destroy us. However, we are not defenseless. By embracing God's character of love, setting boundaries through confession and repentance, and seeking His protection, we can overcome the enemy's attacks. Our faith in God's divine intervention safeguards us, allowing us to live victoriously.

4. The Power of the Occult and Astral Projection:
- Astral projection is a practice rooted in the power of the devil and his evil angels.
- Those who engage in astral projection gain access to homes through objects that belong to the devil.
- Reflective Question: What objects or influences in your life might be granting the enemy access?

Scripture Reference: Ephesians 6:12 - "For we do not wrestle against flesh and blood, but against principalities, against powers, against the rulers of the darkness of this age, against spiritual hosts of wickedness in the heavenly places."

5. Surrendering to God and Separating from Worldly Influences:
- Making a total surrender to the Lord involves distancing ourselves from worldly entertainment and influences.
- Removing objects that separate us from God can lead to remarkable spiritual breakthroughs.
- Reflective Question: What worldly influences or possessions can you eliminate to draw closer to God?

Scripture Reference: James 4:7 - "Submit yourselves therefore to God. Resist the devil, and he will flee from you."

6. Breaking Free from Spiritual Bondage:
- Just as Jesus liberated the woman bound by Satan for 18 years, we too can break free from spiritual bondages.
- Satan gains access through our indulgence in sin, intemperance, and unguarded moments.
- Reflective Question: How can you strengthen your defenses against Satan's access points in your life?

Scripture Reference: 1 Peter 5:8 - "Be sober-minded; be watchful. Your adversary the devil prowls around like a roaring lion, seeking someone to devour."

7. Closing the Doors to Satan's Access:
- Satan's embassy is sin, and wherever sin resides, his rules and regulations prevail.
- By guarding our minds, abstaining from practices that blunt our conscience, and avoiding temptation, we can close the door to Satan's access.
- Reflective Question: How can you fortify your mind and lifestyle to protect against Satan's influence?

Scripture Reference: Psalm 119:11 - "I have stored up your word in my heart, that I might not sin against you."

We will explore various areas where Satan can find footholds, and how we can fortify ourselves against his schemes. Let us anchor our understanding in biblical principles and scriptural references, seeking to grow stronger in our faith and relationship with God.

I. Recognizing Occult Involvement: The enemy seeks to exploit our involvement in occult practices. Reflect upon the following points, reiterating the main ideas:

1. Definition of occult involvement:
   - Occult practices encompass a wide range of activities associated with witchcraft, supernatural phenomena, and spiritual manipulation.
   - Examples include amulets, fortune-telling, magic rituals, psychic consultations, and involvement in occult games.
2. Biblical standpoint on occult involvement:
   - Leviticus 19:31 emphasizes the importance of avoiding mediums and familiar spirits.
   - Deuteronomy 18:10-12 highlights God's prohibition of witchcraft, sorcery, and divination.

Reflective Questions:
- Have you ever been involved in occult practices, either knowingly or unknowingly?
- How can you discern and distance yourself from occult influences?

II. Understanding Occult Phenomena: The enemy may manifest through supernatural occurrences. Reiterate the main points:

1. Examples of occult phenomena:
   - Demonic nightmares, extra sensory perception (ESP), and unexplained disappearances of objects.

- Sensing the presence of evil, hearing unusual sounds or voices, or witnessing ghostly apparitions.

2. Seeking God's protection:
    - Psalm 91:4 assures us of God's shelter and refuge during spiritual battles.
    - Ephesians 6:11-12 emphasizes the importance of wearing the whole armor of God to withstand the enemy's schemes.

Reflective Questions:
- Have you ever experienced any occult phenomena? If so, how did it affect you spiritually?
- How can you rely on God's protection and spiritual armor to combat occult influences?

III. Guarding Against False Teachings: False teachings can pave the way for the enemy's influence. Reinforce the key concepts:

1. Identification of false teachings:
    - Various religious beliefs and practices that contradict biblical truth.
    - Examples include cults, Eastern religions, New Age philosophies, and distorted versions of Christianity.
2. Staying rooted in God's Word:
    - 2 Timothy 3:16-17 emphasizes the Scripture's role in teaching, rebuking, correcting, and training in righteousness.
    - Acts 17:11 encourages us to examine teachings against the Word of God for discernment.

Reflective Questions:
- Have you encountered any false teachings in your life? How did they impact your faith?
- How can you deepen your understanding of biblical truth to safeguard against false doctrines?

IV. Overcoming the Effects of Drug Use: The enemy gains access through mind-altering substances. Reiterate the main ideas:

1. Examples of mind-altering substances:
    - Alcohol, drugs, and other substances that impair judgment, alter perceptions, or induce addictive behaviors.
2. Finding freedom in Christ:
    - 1 Corinthians 6:19-20 reminds us that our bodies are temples of the Holy Spirit, urging us to honor God with them.
    - Galatians 5:1 encourages us to stand firm in the freedom Christ has given us, breaking the bondage of worldly dependencies.

Reflective Questions:

- Have you or your loved ones struggled with substance abuse? How has it affected your spiritual well-being?
- How can you rely on God's strength and support to overcome the allure of mind-altering substances?

V. Discerning Harmful Entertainment: The enemy can use worldly entertainment to infiltrate our lives. Reinforce the key concepts:

1. Types of harmful entertainment:
    - Books, movies, music, social media, and other media that promote ungodly values, immorality, or distorted perspectives.
2. Cultivating discernment and wise choices:
    - Philippians 4:8 encourages us to focus on what is true, noble, just, pure, lovely, and praiseworthy.
    - Romans 12:2 urges us to renew our minds and align our desires with God's will, guarding against conformity to the world.

Reflective Questions:

- How has entertainment influenced your thoughts and behaviors? Are there any specific areas where you need to exercise discernment?
- How can you intentionally choose media that aligns with biblical principles and nourishes your spiritual growth?

NOTE

NOTE

CHAPTER 10:
A LOVE THAT TAKES

In this study guide, we will delve into the topic of "A Love that Takes" based on the book The Law of Life. As Christians, we understand that God is our ultimate source of love, guidance, and fulfillment. Through exploring key concepts and biblical references, we will discover how to come to God, take from His love, and apply it to our lives. Let's dive in!

Main Points:

1. Recognizing God as the Only Source:
    - Emphasize the need to view God as our primary source for love and fulfillment.
    - Encourage readers to turn to God in prayer, expressing their thoughts, feelings, struggles, and desires.
    - Discuss the PRAY acronym (Praise, Repent, Ask, Yield) as a framework for meaningful prayer.
    - Highlight the importance of reading and studying the Bible, as it contains God's love letters and answers to our questions.
    - Encourage daily contemplation on God's love, particularly through meditating on Jesus' sacrifice on the cross.

Scripture References: Psalm 119:105, 2 Corinthians 3:18, John 3:16, Romans 5:8

Reflective Questions:

- How often do you communicate with God through prayer?
- What obstacles prevent you from spending more time reading and studying the Bible?
- How can you prioritize daily reflection on God's love and sacrifice in your life?

2. God as the Sole Source:
    - Affirm that God alone is the true source of acceptance, security, belonging, and love.
    - Contrast human relationships with our relationship with God, emphasizing that others are not meant to be our ultimate sources.
    - Share relevant Bible verses that highlight God's greatness and creative power.
    - Encourage readers to seek acceptance, belonging, security, and harmony from God rather than relying solely on human relationships.

Scripture References: Isaiah 37:16, Psalm 86:10, Colossians 1:15-17

Reflective Questions:

- Do you find yourself seeking acceptance, security, and love primarily from human relationships?
- How can you shift your focus to rely more on God as your ultimate source in these areas?
- Reflect on a time when you experienced true acceptance or security from God. How did it impact your life?

3. Trusting in God's Promises:
    - Highlight the importance of trusting in God's promises to meet our needs.
    - Explore specific promises related to acceptance, belonging, and security.
    - Encourage readers to internalize these promises and rely on them during challenging times.

Scripture References: John 1:12, Acts 10:35, Ephesians 1:3-6, Isaiah 43:1, Philippians 4:19

Reflective Questions:

- Which specific promises from God's Word resonate with you the most?
- How can you remind yourself of these promises daily and lean on them during difficult circumstances?
- Share an experience when God's faithfulness to His promises brought you comfort and assurance.

Through scriptures and reflective questions, we will delve into the promises God has made to us, the transformative power of His love, and the steps we can take to embrace His love fully. Let us embark on this journey of understanding, truth, forgiveness, joy, peace, compassion, and hope.

1. The Need for Understanding: Scripture Reference: Isaiah 53:4; Hebrews 4:15,16
- Reiterate: God empathizes with our weaknesses and invites us to approach His throne of grace to find mercy and help in times of need.
- Reflective Questions:
    1. How does knowing that God understands our weaknesses affect our relationship with Him?
    2. How can we boldly approach God's throne of grace in times of struggle or pain?
2. The Need for Truth: Scripture Reference: Psalm 119:160; John 14:6
- Reiterate: God's Word is truth, and Jesus is the way, the truth, and the life. Through Him, we can find freedom and knowledge of the truth.
- Reflective Questions:

1. How does the truth found in God's Word impact our lives?
2. How can we abide in God's Word and experience the freedom it brings?

3. The Need for Forgiveness: Scripture Reference: Psalm 103:10-12; 1 John 1:9

- Reiterate: God forgives our sins and removes them from us, showing His mercy and compassion. Through confession, He cleanses us from unrighteousness.
- Reflective Questions:
    1. How does God's forgiveness impact our relationship with Him and others?
    2. How can we experience the freedom and peace that come from receiving God's forgiveness?

4. The Need for Joy: Scripture Reference: Psalm 16:11; John 15:11

- Reiterate: In God's presence, there is fullness of joy. His Word brings joy and rejoicing to our hearts. Jesus desires His joy to remain in us and for our joy to be full.
- Reflective Questions:
    1. How can we find joy in God's presence and His Word?
    2. How can we maintain joy in challenging circumstances?

5. The Need for Peace: Scripture Reference: Psalm 29:11; John 14:27

- Reiterate: God blesses His people with peace. Trusting in Him and keeping our minds focused on Him bring perfect peace. Jesus has overcome the world, and through Him, we can find peace.
- Reflective Questions:
    1. How can we experience God's peace in our lives?
    2. How can we trust in God and find peace amidst trials and tribulations?

6. The Need for Compassion: Scripture Reference: Psalm 86:15; Matthew 9:36

- Reiterate: God is full of compassion, gracious, longsuffering, and merciful. Jesus was moved with compassion for the weary and scattered. We are called to show compassion to others as well.
- Reflective Questions:
    1. How can we reflect God's compassion in our interactions with others?
    2. How does understanding God's compassion impact our own lives?

7. The Need for Hope (continued): Scripture Reference: Jeremiah 29:11; John 14:1-3

- Reiterate: God's thoughts toward us are of peace and hope. Jesus promises a place for us in His Father's house, where there is eternal hope and glory.
- Reflective Questions:

1. How does the hope we have in God's promises impact our perspective and choices in life?
2. How can we cultivate and maintain a mindset of hope in challenging times?

Need for redemption, and the transformative power of faith. Through biblical references and reflective questions, we will reinforce the main points and inspire a deeper understanding of this incredible love.

Main Points:

1. A Donor with a Good Heart (Scripture: Jeremiah 17:9; Ezekiel 11:19):
   - To undergo a heart transplant, a suitable donor with a good heart is essential.
   - God, in His infinite love, recognized that His heart was the only one that could save us.

2. The Donor Must Die (Scripture: John 3:16; Romans 5:8):
   - The former owner of the heart must die for the transplant to take place.
   - Jesus, motivated by His deep love for us, willingly sacrificed His life as the perfect donor.

3. The Recipient Must Die and Be Revived (Scripture: Galatians 2:20; Romans 6:4):
   - The recipient of the new heart must undergo a death and revival process.
   - Just as a surgeon replaces the heart, Jesus removes our old heart of sin and offers us new life.

4. Following the Surgeon's Instructions (Scripture: John 14:15; Romans 8:9-11):
   - After a successful transplant, the recipient must diligently follow the Surgeon's instructions.
   - Our new heart, given by God, requires a transformed lifestyle based on His Word and guidance.

Reflective Questions:

1. How does understanding the sacrificial nature of Jesus' death on the cross deepen your appreciation for His love?
2. Reflect on a time when you experienced God's transformative power in your life. How did it feel to be revived?
3. In what ways can you actively follow the instructions of the Great Physician, allowing His heart to guide your actions and choices?

Conclusion: The love of God displayed through the analogy of a heart transplant evokes deep emotions and awakens our spirits to the magnitude of His sacrifice. By accepting His gift of a new heart through faith, we experience a profound transformation. Let us continually reflect on this love, follow the Surgeon's instructions, and walk in the fullness of the new life He has given us.

Scripture References:

- Jeremiah 17:9
- Ezekiel 11:19
- John 3:16
- Romans 5:8
- Galatians 2:20
- Romans 6:4
- John 14:15
- Romans 8:9-11
- Ezekiel 36:26
- Hebrews 11:1

NOTE

NOTE

CHAPTER 11:
A LOVE THAT VALUES

In this study guide, we will explore the profound concept of "A Love that Values" based on the book "THE LAW OF LIFE." As Christians, we seek to understand and embrace the love of God, rooted in biblical teachings. This guide aims to reinforce the main points of the content, provide scriptural references, and offer reflective questions to deepen our understanding and strengthen our faith.

ACCEPTING THE DIVINE EXCHANGE AT THE CROSS

Reiterating the Main Points:

- Through faith, we participate in the divine exchange at the cross, where we receive Jesus' past as our own, and He takes our burdens.
- It's essential to leave our burdens at the cross, trusting that God will work things out according to His infinite love and power.

Reflective Questions:

- How often do you find yourself taking back burdens that you've brought to the Lord in prayer? Why is it challenging to fully trust God?
- How can the concept of the divine exchange at the cross impact the way you approach and surrender your burdens to God?
- What specific steps can you take to leave your burdens at the cross and cultivate a deeper trust in God's love and power?

UNDERSTANDING OUR VALUE IN GOD'S EYES

Reiterating the Main Points:

- The true value of something is determined by what someone is willing to pay for it.
- We are reminded of the vastness and grandeur of the universe, emphasizing God's greatness and power.
- God's promise to Abraham highlights the magnitude of His love and His desire to bless and multiply His people.

Reflective Questions:

- How does contemplating the immense size and complexity of the universe impact your understanding of God's greatness and love?
- In what ways do you underestimate your own value and worth in God's eyes?
- How can you cultivate a deeper appreciation for God's promise to bless and multiply your life, as He did for Abraham?

ENVISIONING HEAVEN'S GLORY

Reiterating the Main Points:

- Imagine the breathtaking beauty and grandeur of heaven, described symbolically in the book of Revelation.
- Heaven is a place where God's glory shines brilliantly, where perfection and harmony abound.
- Reflect on the desire to be in God's presence and the eternal joy that awaits us in heaven.

Reflective Questions:

- How does meditating on the description of heaven inspire your hope and longing for eternal life with God?
- How can the anticipation of heaven influence your perspective on life's challenges and struggles?
- What steps can you take to live with an eternal perspective, keeping heaven in mind as you navigate your daily life?

Imagine the grandeur of God, surrounded by adoring beings, praised for His holiness and love. He is the creator of the universe, speaking everything into existence with His powerful words (Psalm 33:6). Yet, amidst this cosmic scale, let's focus on two tiny creatures on a small planet who rebelled against God. Despite their insignificance, God chose to become one of them, to rescue and redeem them from their rebellion (John 3:16). This study guide explores the profound love that values each soul, as depicted in the book The Law of Life.

Main Points:

1. God's Great Plan:
- Despite our rebellion, God chose to become human to restore friendship with us.
- God's infinite nature encapsulated in the vulnerability of a single cell in Mary's womb.
- Jesus' journey from conception to birth, reflecting God's love and humility.

2. Jesus' Unrecognized Mission:
   - Jesus lived a life of love, constantly seeking to bless and restore others.
   - Misunderstood, suspected, and hated by religious leaders.
   - The world failed to grasp the significance of His true identity and purpose.

3. The Ultimate Sacrifice:
   - Jesus' mission required Him to pay the penalty for humanity's sins.
   - He endured physical torture, mockery, and crucifixion.
   - The greatest suffering was the separation from His Father.

4. The Worth of a Soul:
   - Each individual is worth the life of Christ, as demonstrated by His sacrifice.
   - Humanity's cumulative accomplishments throughout history pale in comparison to the potential of a single saved soul in eternity.
   - God paid the price for each person because He recognized their immeasurable worth.

5. Treating Yourself and Others:
   - Understanding our value as recipients of Christ's sacrifice should change how we treat ourselves.
   - Our bodies are temples of the Holy Spirit, and we should honor God in our actions (1 Corinthians 6:19-20).
   - Recognizing the worth of others, regardless of their circumstances, enables us to love, respect, and sacrifice for their restoration.

Reflective Questions:
1. How does contemplating God's incredible love for us impact your understanding of your own worth?
2. In what ways can you honor God in your body and spirit, considering that you are worth the life of Christ?
3. How can you demonstrate love and respect for others, recognizing their immeasurable worth in Christ?
4. Take a moment to meditate on the suffering and sacrifice Jesus endured for you. How does this deepen your appreciation for His love?

Consider the value of a single soul in eternity. How does this perspective influence your interactions with others and your desire for their restoration?

NOTE

NOTE

CHAPTER 12:
A LOVE THAT SURRENDERS

In this study guide we will explore the concept of A love that Surrenders based on the book "The Law of Life". It is extremely important that as Christians, we exercise complete faith in God. This kind of faith will ensure the spiritual transformation which will enable us to overcome our fears and totally surrender to God. So, dig deep into this guide and know that you will be the overcomer that God created us to be.

Main Points:

1. Surrendering our lives entirely to Jesus is essential for spiritual transformation.
   - The story of Charles Blondin crossing Niagara Falls demonstrates the concept of surrender.
   - Jesus offers to bring us across the chasm of sin, but we need to exercise faith and surrender control.
   - Surrendering means giving up our addictions, fears, and desires to fully trust in God.

2. The decision to surrender: Trusting God completely.
   - Personal testimony of the author's struggle with addictions and the turning point of surrender.
   - Trusting God's ability to save us even when we doubt His faithfulness.
   - Surrendering involves giving up control and trusting God's guidance.

3. Getting into the wheelbarrow: Embracing complete reliance on God.
   - Overcoming challenges and struggles by surrendering to God's will.
   - Encouragement to examine personal areas of struggle and invite God's intervention.
   - Emphasizing the necessity of relying on God rather than personal efforts.

4. Crossing from defeat to victory: Understanding the vast canyon.
   - Recognizing the vast divide between our attempts to overcome and the victorious Christian life.
   - Prayer, scripture reading, service, and obedience alone cannot bridge the divide.
   - Jesus, through His perfect life and sacrificial death, provides the means to cross the canyon.

5. Trusting Jesus completely: Faith in the wheelbarrow.
   - The wheelbarrow symbolizes complete trust and surrender to Jesus.
   - The land of victory involves trust in Jesus rather than self-effort.
   - Challenging readers to identify what they are not willing to surrender for true freedom.

Scripture References:
- Ephesians 2:8-9 - "For by grace you have been saved through faith. And this is not your own doing; it is the gift of God, not a result of works, so that no one may boast."
- Proverbs 3:5-6 - "Trust in the Lord with all your heart, and do not lean on your own understanding. In all your ways acknowledge him, and he will make straight your paths."
- Matthew 16:24 - "Then Jesus said to his disciples, 'If anyone would come after me, let him deny himself and take up his cross and follow me.'"

Reflective Questions:
1. What are the areas in your life where you struggle to surrender control to God? How can you invite Him into those areas?
2. Have you experienced moments of doubt about God's faithfulness? How can you grow in trust and fully rely on Him?
3. What is holding you back from getting into the "wheelbarrow" of faith? What sacrifices are you unwilling to make?
4. How does the concept of surrender challenge your understanding of personal effort and relying on God's grace?
5. Reflect on a time when you experienced victory through complete trust in Jesus. How did that impact your faith journey?

Remember, surrendering to God's love and fully trusting in Him is the key to experiencing spiritual transformation and victory in life. Embrace the journey of surrender, relying on His strength, and enjoy the ride as He leads you to the land of victory.

In the journey of faith, surrendering ourselves completely to God is both a challenging and transformative decision. It requires us to let go of control and place our trust fully in Jesus. This study guide explores the concept of surrender based on the book "The Law of Life" and emphasizes its significance from a biblical perspective. Let us dive into this study and discover the joy and freedom found in surrendering to God's perfect love.

Main Points:
1. Surrendering to Christ:
   - Surrender is an act of faith, entrusting our lives entirely to Jesus.

- It involves giving up our own desires, plans, and aspirations, aligning ourselves with God's will.
- Surrender requires a willingness to face challenges, ridicule, and even death for the sake of Christ.

Scripture references: Matthew 16:24, Luke 9:23, Romans 12:1

Reflective Question: How can you demonstrate your willingness to surrender completely to Christ in your daily life?

2. The Consequences of Self-Reliance:
   - Without surrendering to Christ, we remain lost and defeated, regardless of external appearances.
   - Our own efforts and righteousness cannot save us or bring us to a place of victory.
   - Recognizing our inability to save ourselves is crucial for embracing the need for surrender.

Scripture references: Romans 3:12, Romans 3:23, Matthew 19:17, Isaiah 64:6

Reflective Question: How has self-reliance hindered your spiritual growth and victory in the past?

3. The Benefits of Surrender:
   - Surrendering to Christ opens the doors to victory, perfect love, peace, and freedom.
   - In surrender, we find forgiveness, freedom from the past, and eternal life.
   - Jesus dwells with us, guiding and transforming our lives as we abide in Him.

Scripture references: John 10:10, Galatians 5:22-23, Isaiah 55:8-9

Reflective Question: How have you experienced the transformative power of surrender in your life?

4. Surrendering Without Reservation:
   - Surrendering is not merely a desire or intellectual agreement but actively letting go.
   - We must trust God even when we don't fully understand the consequences or have all the answers.
   - Delaying obedience or seeking complete understanding before surrendering hinders our freedom.

Scripture references: Luke 9:62, Proverbs 3:5-6

Reflective Question: In what areas of your life are you hesitant to surrender completely to God? How can you overcome this hesitation?

5. Surrender as Taking up the Cross:
    - Taking up the cross means surrendering our own desires and plans to follow Christ.
    - Surrendering is about allowing Christ to direct our lives, surpassing our own limited expectations.
    - Through surrender, we are grafted into Christ, and His character begins to manifest in us.

Scripture references: Luke 9:23, Galatians 2:20, John 15:4-5

Reflective Question: How can you daily take up your cross and surrender your life to Christ?

Conclusion: Surrendering ourselves completely to Christ is an act of faith that brings profound transformation and freedom. Through surrender, we experience the love, joy, peace, and righteousness that God offers us. Let us embrace the challenge of surrender, trusting that Jesus will guide us on a journey filled with purpose, victory, and an intimate relationship with Him.

Scripture reference: Romans 6:13

Reflective Question: What steps will you take to deepen your surrender to Christ and experience the fullness of his holiness?

NOTE

NOTE

CHAPTER 13:
A LOVE THAT THINKS WELL

The book "The Law of Life" explores the concept of surrendering our hearts to God's love and understanding the transformative power it can have in our lives. In this study guide, we will delve into the key insights from the book and explore how biblical principles can guide us towards surrendering our hearts to God's love. Through reflective questions and scriptural references, we aim to deepen our understanding and strengthen our spiritual connection.

1. Searching the Heart:
- Our hearts can be deceitful, and we need to search them earnestly (Psalm 139:23- 24).

- Trials reveal what is truly in our hearts, as our response reflects our inner disposition (Matthew 12:34).

- Reflective Question: How have trials in your life revealed what is in your heart? How did you respond?

2. The Body's Reflection:
- The body carries a faithful record of what has been done to it, exposing the impact of our hearts on our physical well-being.

- Our thoughts and emotions can manifest in physical ailments.
- Reflective Question: Have you observed any connection between your thoughts/emotions and your physical health? How can you align your heart and body in God's healing?

3. Treasuring the Right Things:
- Our treasures reveal the state of our hearts and what we prioritize (Matthew 6:21).

- Our time, money, and conversations indicate where our treasure lies.
- Reflective Question: What are the primary treasures in your life? How can you align them with God's priorities?

4. Setting Our Minds on the Spirit:
- Living according to the Spirit requires focusing our minds on spiritual things (Romans 8:5).
- Spending time with God in nature helps open our hearts to Him.
- Reflective Question: How can you prioritize spending time with God in nature? How does it impact your connection with Him?

5. Understanding Legitimate Needs and Deception:
- Examining our thoughts, words, and actions, we can identify legitimate needs and how our hearts deceive us.
- Recognizing our need for acceptance and belonging from God, rather than seeking it from others.
- Reflective Question: Can you recall a situation where your heart deceived you? How can you rely on God's acceptance and belonging?

6. Choosing Positive Thoughts:
- Thinking positively about others, even those who have hurt us, can bring healing and transformation.
- Asking God to help us see others through His eyes and to love them as He does.
- Keeping a list of what God loves about them and choosing to think upon that list whenever "they" come to mind.
- Reflective Question: Is there someone in your life whom you find it difficult to think positively about? How can you seek God's perspective and love for them?

7. Escaping the Bitterness Trap:
- Recognizing that God is just and administers justice for the sake of others, not selfishly.
- Bitterness arises from a misguided sense of justice, where we try to extract penalties from others.
- Bitterness as a prison cell: Holding others captive in bitterness only keeps ourselves imprisoned.
- Realizing the deception: We are responsible to God, not to others, and bitterness locks us inside the cell.
- The key to freedom: Forgiveness breaks the chains of bitterness and sets us free.
- Reflective Questions: Have you ever struggled with bitterness? How can you surrender

your sense of justice to God's perfect justice? How does the divine exchange at the cross impact your forgiveness of others?

Key Scriptures:
1. Romans 12:19 - "Beloved, never avenge yourselves, but leave it to the wrath of God, for it is written, 'Vengeance is mine, I will repay, says the Lord.'"
2. Philippians 2:5 - "Let this mind be in you which was also in Christ Jesus."
3. Philippians 4:8 - "Finally, brothers and sisters, whatever is true, whatever is noble, whatever is right, whatever is pure, whatever is lovely, whatever is admirable—if anything is excellent or praiseworthy—think about such things."
4. Luke 19:13 - "So he called ten of his servants and gave them ten minas. 'Put this money to work,' he said, 'until I come back.'"

Main Points:
1. Bitterness and its Deception
- Bitterness is like a prison cell, where we hold others captive for their wrongdoings.
- By assuming the role of God, we unknowingly imprison ourselves.
- We cannot be free unless we release others and understand our debt is to God, not others.

2. The Key of Forgiveness
- Forgiveness is the key to open the prison cell of bitterness.
- Holding onto hurt feelings does not bring justice; it only prolongs our suffering.
- The foundation of bitterness is flawed and contrary to God's true nature.

3. The Proper Foundation for Forgiveness
- Recognizing that what others did to us is ultimately against God, not us.
- Jesus took our place on the cross, becoming the victim for our sins.
- Our debt is to God, and true forgiveness starts with accepting His love and extending it to others.

4. Overcoming Negative Thoughts
- The mind was created to be occupied, not emptied.
- Displacement Principle: Focusing on positive thoughts replaces negative ones.
- Meditate on God's promises, contemplate His love, and fill the mind with His Word.

Reflective Questions:

1. Have you ever experienced the prison of bitterness? How did it affect you?
2. How does understanding that your debt is to God, not others, change your perspective on forgiveness?
3. What scriptures can you meditate on to replace negative thoughts with positive, faith-filled ones?
4. Share a personal experience where forgiveness and letting go of bitterness brought freedom and healing.

OVERCOME NEGATIVE THOUGHTS, FIND FREEDOM FROM GUILT, AND ALLOW GOD'S LOVE TO SHAPE OUR LIVES.

I. Overcoming Negative Thoughts:

1. The Battle of Negative Thoughts:

- The author's personal struggle with addiction and negative thoughts.
- The use of 3X5 cards as a tool to overcome negative thoughts.
- The initial difficulty and the perseverance required. Scripture: Philippians 4:8, Romans 12:2 Reflective Question: How can you apply the practice of using affirmations and God's promises to overcome negative thoughts in your own life?

2. The Victory of Overcoming:
- Reaching a point of victory over negative thoughts.
- Realizing the absence of negative thoughts throughout the day.

- Discovering that dreams gradually align with conscious experiences. Scripture: Psalm 51:10, Isaiah 43:18-19 Reflective Question: How can you apply the principle of overcoming negative thoughts to experience true victory and renewal in your own life?

II. Embracing God's Love:

1. Recognizing God's Everlasting Love:
- The lie of feeling unloved and countering it with biblical truth.
- God's promise of everlasting love and His kind and merciful nature. Scripture:

Jeremiah 31:3, Romans 8:38-39 Reflective Question: How can you remind yourself daily of God's everlasting love and let it transform your self-perception?

2. Overcoming Guilt and Shame:
- Differentiating between specific guilt tied to sin and general guilt.
- Confessing specific sins to God and seeking forgiveness.
- Understanding the importance of repentance and turning away from sin. Scripture: 1 John 1:9, Psalm 32:5 Reflective Question: How can you embrace God's forgiveness and avoid falling into the trap of general guilt that separates you from Him?

III. The Power of Choice:
1. Train of Life:
- Understanding life as a train driven by choices and influenced by feelings.
- Satan's attempt to manipulate feelings and redirect our choices.
- Choosing to follow God regardless of our feelings. Scripture: Proverbs 3:5-6, Romans 8:6 Reflective Question: How can you prioritize making choices aligned with God's will, even when your feelings may be pulling you in a different direction?

2. The Law of the Mind:
- The transformative power of focus and beholding.
- Choosing what to think about to shape our character.
- Deliberately focusing on the love and righteousness of God. Scripture: 2 Corinthians 3:18, Philippians 4:8 Reflective Question: How can you actively apply the law of the mind to align your thoughts with God's love and goodness, transforming your character?

SENSES VS. FEELINGS

Separating Senses and Feelings

1. What is the difference between senses and feelings?
2. How can we control our emotional reactions to external stimuli?
3. Provide an example of a situation where you can choose a positive emotional response despite negative stimuli.
4. Reflect on 2 Corinthians 3:18 and explain its significance in understanding the transformation of our feelings through surrender.

Controlling Inputs and Outputs

1. Why is it important to carefully consider how we spend our time, interests, efforts, and resources?
2. Compare the time you spend on spiritual activities (scripture study, prayer, helping others) with the time spent on worldly distractions (TV, social media, entertainment). What changes can you make to prioritize spiritual inputs?
3. Reflect on Philippians 4:8. How can meditating on virtuous and praiseworthy things influence our emotional responses?
4. Discuss the idea that cheerfulness and thankfulness are choices rather than products of circumstances. How can you actively cultivate these attitudes in your life?

Resting in Christ's Transforming Love

1. Explain the concept of a life in Christ as a life of restfulness.
2. How does focusing on Christ's love, character, and self-denial help us overcome negative thoughts and emotions?
3. Reflect on the challenge of forgiveness and taking every thought captive to Christ's obedience. How can you find hope and faithfulness in this process?
4. Meditate on Hebrews 10:23. How does God's faithfulness assure us that we can overcome and surrender our feelings to His transforming power?

Key Points:

1. Our senses perceive stimuli from the world, while our feelings are our emotional responses to those stimuli.
2. By surrendering our feelings to God's will, we can choose positive emotional responses despite negative circumstances.
3. We have the power to control our inputs (what we expose ourselves to) and outputs (how we respond emotionally).
4. Philippians 4:8 guides us to meditate on virtuous and praiseworthy things, shaping our emotional responses.
5. Choosing cheerfulness and thankfulness is possible through our reliance on Christ's strength and character.
6. The process of surrendering our feelings and taking every thought captive requires hope, faithfulness, and trust in God's faithfulness.

Scriptures:

- 2 Corinthians 3:18: "And we all, who with unveiled faces contemplate the Lord's glory, are being transformed into his image with ever-increasing glory, which comes from the Lord, who is the Spirit."

- 1 Thessalonians 5:18: "Give thanks in all circumstances; for this is God's will for you in Christ Jesus."

- Philippians 4:8: "Finally, brothers and sisters, whatever is true, whatever is noble, whatever is right, whatever is pure, whatever is lovely, whatever is admirable—if anything is excellent or praiseworthy—think about such things."

- Hebrews 10:23: "Let us hold unswervingly to the hope we profess, for he who promised is faithful."

Reflective Questions:

1. How can you actively practice surrendering your feelings to God's will in your daily life?

2. Are there specific areas in your life where you struggle to control your emotional responses? How can you seek God's help in those areas?

3. How has meditating on virtuous and praiseworthy things impacted your emotional well-being?

4. In what ways can you rest in Christ's love and find peace amidst challenging circumstances?

Rundown: As we surrender our feelings to God's transformative love, we discover the power to choose positive emotional responses, control our inputs and outputs, and rest in the assurance of His faithfulness. By reflecting on the Scriptures and incorporating them into our lives, we can experience the profound transformation that comes from surrendering our feelings to God. Embrace His love, trust His guidance, and allow His Spirit to shape your emotions for His glory.

NOTE

NOTE

CHAPTER 14:
A LOVE THAT GIVES ALL

In Chapter 14 of this Study Guide based on the Book "The Law of Life", we will take another concept of Love as presented by the author. Looking deeply in the Word of God, the author finds scriptures and stories which to understand the concept which focuses on A Love that gives all. The author also shares real life stories of individuals who have learned what it takes to give all. It is God's love which He freely gives, to all believers which will enable us to love others. Take the dive into this chapter and learn how to love even when it hurts, even when it seems unfair and so fulfill God's greatest commandment – to love and not count the cost.

Main Points:

1. Love Others:
- Treat others with love in thoughts, words, and actions.
- Allow the Holy Spirit to work through us, becoming conduits of God's love.
- Remember that people's hurtful actions were directed towards Jesus, not us.
- Share the story of Adelle Selfu's forgiveness and ministry to her husband's killer.

Scripture References:

- John 13:34-35: "A new command I give you: Love one another. As I have loved you, so you must love one another. By this, everyone will know that you are my disciples if you love one another."

- Matthew 5:44: "But I tell you, love your enemies and pray for those who persecute you."

Reflective Questions:

1. How can we demonstrate love to others in our thoughts, words, and actions?
2. How does remembering that people hurt Jesus, not us, help us show love and forgiveness?
3. Are there any areas in your life where you need to let go of bitterness and anger?
4. How can the story of Adelle Selfu inspire us to extend forgiveness and minister to others?

Main Points: 2. The Law and the Heart:
- The Law of Life can only come from a transformed heart by God's grace.
- Divine love, motivated by God's heart, allows us to keep God's commandments.
- Operating with human love and selfish motives hinders us from obeying God's law.
- Surrendering ourselves to God and allowing the Holy Spirit to work within us enables us to keep His commandments.

Scripture References:
- Jeremiah 31:33: "I will put my law in their minds and write it on their hearts. I will be their God, and they will be my people."
- Romans 13:10: "Love does no harm to a neighbor. Therefore love is the fulfillment of the law."

Reflective Questions:
1. How does a transformed heart by God's grace enable us to keep His commandments?
2. In what ways does human love and selfish motives hinder our obedience to God's law?
3. How can we surrender ourselves to God and allow the Holy Spirit to work within us?
4. Reflect on areas in your life where you can grow in obeying God's commandments through His love.

Main Points: 3. Love & Liberty:
- Human love tends to control when there is high interest, while low interest allows freedom.
- Divine love operates differently, giving freedom and allowing others to be themselves.
- Recognizing that everything we have belongs to God helps us love without controlling others.

Scripture References:
- Galatians 5:13: "You, my brothers and sisters, were called to be free. But do not use your freedom to indulge the flesh; rather, serve one another humbly in love."
- 1 Peter 4:8: "Above all, love each other deeply because love covers over a multitude of sins."

Reflective Questions:
1. How does human love tend to control, while divine love grants freedom?
2. How can recognizing that everything we have belongs to God help us love without controlling others?
3. Are there areas in your relationships where you need to give more freedom and show love unconditionally?
4. How can the concept of love and liberty influence your interactions with others?

Note: Please note that the emotional tone and the specific content related to the book "The Law of Life" and biblical references have been incorporated into the study guide to reinforce understanding, biblical principles, and spiritual reflection.

Let's move next to the importance of freedom in maintaining love and the consequences of our choices. Throughout this guide, we will reinforce key points with relevant scriptures and reflective questions to deepen our understanding.

Main Points:
1. Divine Love and Freedom:
- Divine love allows for maximum interest and total freedom.
- God does not manipulate or force us to love Him.
- We must understand that faith is not a means to control God but a hand to accept His will.
- Scripture Reference: Galatians 5:1 - "For freedom, Christ has set us free; stand firm, therefore, and do not submit again to a yoke of slavery."

2. The Boundaries of Love:
- Love operates within the framework of freedom and boundaries.
- Attempting to control others goes against the principles of love.
- Controlling others, even with good intentions, damages relationships and hinders

personal growth.

- Scripture Reference: 1 Corinthians 16:14 - "Let all that you do be done in love."

3. Consequences and God's Training:
- God, out of His love, allows us to experience consequences for our actions.
- Our decisions have consequences, which God uses to teach, redirect, and restore us.

- God's purpose is not punishment but redemption and restoration.
- Scripture Reference: Galatians 6:7 - "Do not be deceived: God is not mocked, for whatever one sows, that will he also reap."

4. Maintaining Freedom and Standards:
- Freedom does not mean eliminating standards but allowing individual choice.
- Standards are essential for individuals, families, organizations, and governments.
- Authorities enforce consequences for the benefit of the offender and others.
- Scripture Reference: James 1:25 - "But the one who looks into the perfect law, the law of liberty, and perseveres, being no hearer who forgets but a doer who acts, he will be blessed in his doing."

5. Sin and Grace:
- By God's grace, we live and have the power to act.
- Sinning is a misuse of the power God grants us.
- God hates sin but grants us an opportunity for salvation through His grace.
- Scripture Reference: Romans 6:14 - "For sin will have no dominion over you since you are not under law but under grace."

6. Love's Characteristics:
- Exploring the qualities of love as described in 1 Corinthians 13.

- Love suffers long, is kind, does not envy, does not parade itself, is not puffed up, does not behave rudely, does not seek its own, is not provoked.

- Reflecting on how we can embody these characteristics in our relationships.
- Scripture Reference: 1 Corinthians 13:4-7 - "Love is patient and kind; love does not envy or boast; it is not arrogant or rude. It does not insist on its own way; it is not irritable or resentful."

Reflective Questions:

1. How does understanding divine love and freedom impact your perspective on relationships with God and others?

2. Reflect on a time when you tried to control someone for their own good. What were the consequences, and what did you learn from that experience?

3. How can you incorporate the characteristics of love mentioned in 1 Corinthians 13 into your daily interactions?

LET US DELVE FURTHER AND DISCOVER HOW LOVE CAN TRANSFORM OUR LIVES.

Main Points and Scripture References:

1. Emotional Hurts and Unhealed Wounds:
- Our emotional hurts are like buttons that can be easily triggered by certain situations.

- When we have unhealed hurts, we tend to respond negatively to others without understanding why.

- Scripture Reference: "He heals the brokenhearted and binds up their wounds." (Psalm 147:3)

Reflective Question: Have you experienced situations where unhealed emotional hurts influenced your responses?

2. Love Heals All Hurts:
- Love has the power to heal all the hurts from our past.
- When we experience love at the foot of the cross, Jesus takes our hurts and offers us His hurt-free life.

- Scripture Reference: "Above all, love each other deeply, because love covers over a multitude of sins." (1 Peter 4:8)

Reflective Question: How has experiencing God's love transformed your life and healed your emotional wounds?

3. Understanding Others' Pain:
- When someone responds poorly to us, it is often a reflection of their internal pain.

- Instead of reacting negatively, we should respond with gentleness and patience, understanding their hurt.

- Scripture Reference: "Be kind and compassionate to one another, forgiving each other, just as in Christ God forgave you." (Ephesians 4:32)

Reflective Question: How can you show kindness and compassion to someone who responds poorly to you?

4. Positive Thoughts and Compassionate Prayers:
   - Love thinks no evil and assumes the purity of others' motives.
   - We should pray for and work with others, always having positive thoughts about them.
   - Scripture Reference: "Finally, brothers and sisters, whatever is true, whatever is noble, whatever is right, whatever is pure, whatever is lovely, whatever is admirable—if anything is excellent or praiseworthy—think about such things." (Philippians 4:8)

Reflective Question: How can you cultivate positive thoughts about others and pray for their well-being?

5. Love Rejoices in Truth and Endures All Things:
   - Love does not take pleasure in sin or iniquity but rejoices in the truth.
   - Love is able to bear anything and overcome all challenges through God's grace.
   - Scripture Reference: "Love does not delight in evil but rejoices with the truth." (1 Corinthians 13:6)

Reflective Question: How can you cultivate a love that rejoices in truth and endures through challenging circumstances?

6. Love Never Fails:
   - Love, rooted in God's nature, is bound to succeed and triumph over all obstacles.
   - It is through love that we find victory and fulfillment in our lives.
   - Scripture Reference: "And now these three remain: faith, hope and love. But the greatest of these is love." (1 Corinthians 13:13)

Reflective Question: How does knowing that love never fails give you hope and assurance?

NOTE

NOTE

CHAPTER 15:
A LOVE THAT HEALS

The topic of "A Love that Heals" is centered around understanding the transformative power of God's love in our lives. This study guide will explore key concepts from the book "The Law of Life" and reinforce the main points through biblical references and reflective questions. We will delve into the importance of recognizing that everything belongs to God, embracing love, trust, and protection, and understanding the connection between love and disease.

Main Points:

1. Remember, It's Not Mine:
   - We often struggle with treating things, people, and relationships as if they are ours, when in reality, they belong to God.
   - Surrendering control to God and trusting Him in every situation is essential.
   - Reflective Question: How can you remind yourself that everything belongs to God and surrender control to Him?

Scripture References:
   - Psalm 24:1
   - 1 Corinthians 6:19-20
   - Proverbs 3:5-6

2. Love, Trust, and Protection:
   - Love and trust go hand in hand; if we truly love God, we can trust Him completely.
   - Trusting God means we do not need to protect ourselves, as He will protect us according to His wisdom.
   - Reflective Question: How can you deepen your trust in God's protection and demonstrate love to those who oppose or mistreat you?

Scripture References:
- Luke 6:27-36
- Romans 12:19-21

3. Love & Disease:
- Disease is an attempt by our bodies to free themselves from the effects of violating the laws of health.
- Personal loss, driven by the old heart's self-centered love, contributes to physical decline.
- Embracing divine love eliminates loss and prevents its negative impact on our well-being.
- Reflective Question: How can you shift from self-centered love to divine love and experience greater physical and emotional well-being?

Scripture References:
- The Ministry of Healing, page 127
- 1 Corinthians 13:4-7

4. Which Heart Do I Have?
- Contrasting characteristics of the old heart (selfish love) and the new heart (divine love).
- Recognizing the importance of possessing the new heart and its impact on our thoughts and actions.
- Reflective Question: How can you identify the traits of the new heart in your life and actively cultivate divine love?

Scripture References:
- Ezekiel 36:26
- 1 Corinthians 13:1-3

The Old Heart vs. the New Heart
1. According to the book, how does the old heart respond to temptation and trial compared to the new heart?
2. What sets the new heart apart in terms of its capacity to love?
3. How does the new heart handle situations differently than the old heart?
4. Reflect on a personal experience where you witnessed the transformative power of divine love in your own life or someone else's.

The Extraordinary Love of the New Heart
1. How does the new heart demonstrate love towards its enemies?
2. In what ways does the new heart go above and beyond in showing kindness to those who mistreat it?
3. Explore the concept of turning the other cheek and its significance in practicing divine love.
4. Share an example from your life where you found the strength to love someone who treated you poorly.

Giving and Forgiving with the New Heart
1. Contrast the giving nature of the old heart with that of the new heart.
2. How does the new heart respond to requests for help or assistance?
3. Discuss the importance of forgiveness in the context of divine love.
4. Reflect on a situation where you experienced the freedom and peace that comes from forgiving someone.

The Healing Power of Divine Love
1. According to the book, what is the connection between love and disease?
2. How does a lack of divine love contribute to mental and physical ailments?
3. Why is it crucial to identify the cause of our illnesses and adopt a healthy lifestyle?
4. Meditate on 1 Corinthians 13:4-7 and consider how love can bring healing and restoration.

Key Points:
1. The new heart exhibits enduring strength in the face of temptation and trial.
2. Divine love extends to enemies, goes beyond what is expected, and blesses those who curse.
3. The new heart practices forgiveness, generosity, and a willingness to give without expecting anything in return.
4. Love plays a significant role in physical and mental well-being, and adopting a healthy lifestyle is essential.
5. Divine love has the power to heal and restore our hearts, relationships, and overall health.

Scripture References:
- 1 John 4:7-8 - "Dear friends, let us love one another, for love comes from God. Everyone who loves has been born of God and knows God. Whoever does not love does not know God, because God is love."
- Matthew 5:44 - "But I tell you, love your enemies and pray for those who persecute you."
- 1 Corinthians 13:4-7 - "Love is patient, love is kind. It does not envy, it does not boast, it is not proud. It does not dishonor others, it is not self-seeking, it is not easily angered, it keeps no record of wrongs. Love does not delight in evil but rejoices with the truth. It always protects, always trusts, always hopes, always perseveres."

Reflective Questions:
1. How can you cultivate divine love in your daily interactions with others?
2. Are there any specific relationships in your life where you struggle to exhibit divine love? How can you seek healing and restoration in those relationships?
3. What steps can you take to prioritize a healthy lifestyle that supports your physical and mental well-being?
4. How can the transformative power of divine love bring healing to your own heart and contribute to a more loving and compassionate world?

NOTE

NOTE

CHAPTER 16:
A LOVE THAT OBEYS

In chapter 16 of this Study Guide based on the book "The Law of Life" The concept of Obedience is explored. Was Jesus obedient to his Father? Did He willingly do all He was asked to do? This chapter focusses specifically on obedience to God's health laws. In this short Chapter entitled A love that Obeys, the author, shares from The Ministry of Healing by E.G. White. Yes, traditional medicine has a part to play. The writer of the Law of Life, has a degree in Medicine! However as you study this chapter, dear reader, you will undoubtedly, recognize the supreme value of the blessings of a love that operates in obedience to God.

USE NATURAL REMEDIES, CHANGE MY LIFESTYLE

Main Points:

1. Using natural remedies and changing our lifestyle promotes wellness and honors God's gift of our bodies.
2. The Ministry of Healing emphasizes the importance of correcting wrong habits and developing right habits.
3. Natural remedies, such as hydrotherapy, herbs, good food, exercise, and prayer, assist in healing and restoring the body.
4. Our motivation to obey and seek healing should stem from our love for God and our desire to serve Him.
5. The law of cause and effect applies to disease and lifestyle choices, and addressing the cause is essential for true healing.
6. The laws of function, including God's law, are unchangeable and govern the way love functions in our lives.
7. Jesus came not to abolish the law but to fulfill it, providing a perfect sacrifice for our sins.
8. The ceremonial law was nailed to the cross, but the law of love, God's law, remains unchanged.
9. Sin is the transgression of the law, and our obedience to God's law is a reflection of our love for Him.

Scripture References:

1. 1 Corinthians 6:19-20 - "Or do you not know that your body is the temple of the Holy Spirit who is in you, whom you have from God, and you are not your own?

For you were bought at a price; therefore glorify God in your body and in your spirit, which are God's."
2. James 5:14-16 - "Is anyone among you sick? Let him call for the elders of the church, and let them pray over him, anointing him with oil in the name of the Lord. And the prayer of faith will save the sick, and the Lord will raise him up. And if he has committed sins, he will be forgiven. Confess your trespasses to one another, and pray for one another, that you may be healed. The effective, fervent prayer of a righteous man avails much."
3. Exodus 20:2-17 - The Ten Commandments, which reveal the law that governs the function of love.
4. John 14:15, 21 - "If you love Me, keep My commandments... He who has My commandments and keeps them, it is he who loves Me."

Reflective Questions:
1. How does understanding that our bodies are temples of the Holy Spirit impact the way we care for our health?
2. Why is it important to develop right habits and correct wrong habits in areas such as dressing, thinking, eating, and drinking?
3. How can natural remedies and lifestyle changes assist in the healing process and help us establish the right conditions in our bodies?
4. What motivates you to obey God's commands and seek healing? How does divine love differ from human love in our obedience?
5. Why is it crucial to identify and address the cause of a disease or unhealthy lifestyle rather than merely treating the symptoms?
6. How do the unchangeable laws of function, including God's law, govern the way love functions in our lives?
7. Why did Jesus come to fulfill the law? How does His perfect life and sacrifice provide for our past and the penalty of breaking the law?
8. What is the distinction between the ceremonial law and God's law of love? Why was the ceremonial law nailed to the cross?
9. How does sin relate to the transgression of the law? How can we align our lives with God's law and express our love for Him through obedience?

NOTE

NOTE

CHAPTER 17:
A LOVE THAT OVERCOMES

In this study guide, we will explore the theme of "A Love that Overcomes" based on the book "The Law of Life." As Christians, we are called to trust in God's love and rely on His promises. This study guide aims to reinforce our understanding of this concept through biblical references, reflective questions, and key points from the book. Let us delve deeper into the content and discover how we can apply these teachings in our lives.

Main Points:

1. Faith in Jesus and His Word:
   - Jesus gave the lame man by the pool of Bethesda a command: to take up his bed and walk (John 5:2-8).
   - The man had to trust in Jesus, exercise faith, and believe in His words.
   - Faith is essential in our journey of overcoming obstacles and receiving God's blessings.

2. Acting Upon God's Commands:
   - The man, despite having no capacity to accomplish the task, acted upon Jesus' command.
   - Faith without action is ineffective; we need to step out in obedience, even when it seems impossible.
   - When we act upon God's commands, He empowers us to accomplish what He has asked of us.

3. Overcoming the Fear of Failure:
   - We often listen to lies and doubt God's ability to help us overcome.
   - God wants us to trust Him, not ourselves or others' opinions.
   - We must learn to trust in His promises and believe that we can overcome any challenge through His strength.

4. Learning from Falling:
   - Like a baby learning to walk, we may stumble and fall after taking our first steps in faith.
   - Falling is a natural part of the learning process; God does not condemn us for it.

- God's love is patient and understanding, just as parents are when their child falls while learning to walk.

5. The Power of God's Grace:
   - God's grace does not excuse us from concern or encourage willful sin.
   - Understanding the depth of God's love and the sacrifice of Jesus on the cross compels us to walk away from sin.
   - As we grow in Christ, we become more stable and less prone to falling.

Reiteration of Main Points:

1. Trust in Jesus and have faith in His word to overcome challenges.
2. Act upon God's commands, even when it seems impossible, and He will empower us.
3. Overcome the fear of failure and trust that God's love is greater than any obstacle.
4. Learn from our falls and embrace God's patient love as we continue our journey.
5. Embrace the power of God's grace to walk in righteousness and become all that He created us to be.

Reflective Questions:

1. How can we deepen our trust in God and believe in His promises despite the lies we hear?
2. Reflect on a time when you acted upon God's command and experienced His empowerment.
3. How does knowing that God's love is patient and understanding impact your response to failure?
4. How can you grow in Christ and become more stable in your faith?
5. In what ways can you rely on God's grace without taking it for granted?

Scripture References:

- John 5:2-8: The healing of the lame man by the pool of Bethesda.
- Proverbs 24:16: "A righteous man may fall seven times and rise again."
- Matthew 18:22: Jesus' teaching on forgiveness and the importance of getting back up.
- Romans 6:1,2: The balance between God's grace and living in righteousness.

As we embrace the love of God that overcomes, let us remember to trust in Jesus, act upon His commands, and not be discouraged by failure. Through God's grace, we can rise again and continue our journey towards victory. May this study guide inspire you to deepen your faith, overcome obstacles, and experience the blessings that await those who persevere.

NOTE

NOTE

Made in the USA
Middletown, DE
28 December 2023